LEGO NINJAGO
Masters of Spinjitzu

CHARACTER ENCYCLOPEDIA

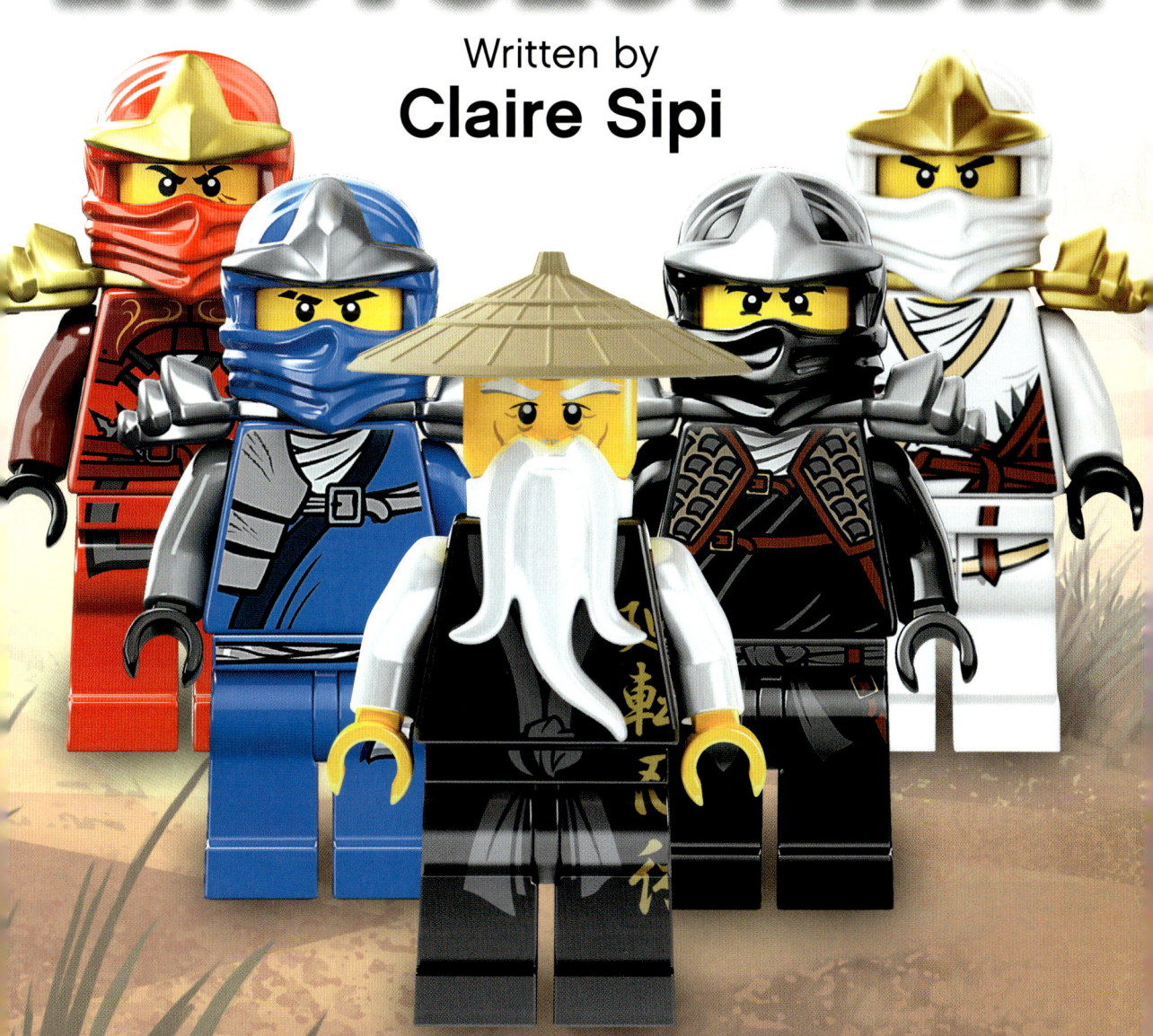

Written by
Claire Sipi

CONTENTS

4	Welcome Brave Ninja	36	Fire Temple	66	Skeleton Bowling
6	History of Ninjago	38	Kai DX	68	Kruncha
		39	Fire Dragon	70	Skullcopter
		40	Jay DX	72	Wyplash

NINJA VS. SKELETON

		41	Lightning Dragon	74	Skull Truck
		42	Cole DX	76	Nuckal
10	Lord Garmadon Returns	43	Earth Dragon	78	Nuckal's ATV
12	Meet The Ninja	44	Zane DX	80	Dark Fortress
14	Ninja Wisdom	45	Ice Dragon	82	Weapons
16	Kai	46	Meet The Skeleton Army	86	Final Battle At The Dark Fortress
18	Nya	48	Skeleton Wisdom		
20	Blacksmith Shop	50	Lord Garmadon		

NINJA VS. SERPENTINE

22	Sensei Wu	51	Samukai		
24	Spinjitzu Dojo	52	Frakjaw		
26	Jay	54	Turbo Shredder	90	A New Adventure
28	Cole	56	Krazi	92	Sensei Wu
30	Zane	58	Chopov	94	Destiny's Bounty
32	Mountain Shrine	60	Skull Motorbike	96	Kai ZX
34	Training Outpost	62	Bonezai	98	Blade Cycle
35	Ambush Shrine	64	Ninja Battle Arena	100	Jay ZX
				102	Storm Fighter

104	Samurai X	138	Fangdam		
106	Samurai Mech	140	Fangpyre Truck	**AND BEYOND...**	
108	Cole ZX	142	Fangpyre Wrecking Ball		
110	Tread Assault			172	Minifigure Gallery
112	Zane ZX	144	Fang-Suei	174	Set Gallery
114	Ultra Sonic Raider	146	Rattlecopter	176	Acknowledgments
116	Kendo Ninja	148	Fangpyre Mech		
117	NRG Ninja	150	Snappa		
118	The Green Ninja	151	Skales		
120	Meet The Serpentine	152	Slithraa		
		153	Rattla		
124	Serpentine Wisdom	154	Mezmo		
126	Lord Garmadon	155	Skalidor		
127	Lloyd Garmadon	156	Bytar		
128	Venomari Shrine	157	Chokun		
130	Acidicus	158	Snike		
131	Spitta	159	Pythor		
132	Lasha	160	Snake Arena		
134	Lasha's Bite Cycle	162	Epic Dragon Battle		
136	Lizaru	164	Weapons		
137	Fangtom	168	Ultra Dragon VS. The Great Devourer		

IF YOU SLITHER OR RATTLE PREPARE TO DO BATTLE!

WELCOME
BRAVE NINJA

The world of LEGO® Ninjago is full of adventure, danger, and epic battles! Meet the four Ninja, Kai, Cole, Jay, and Zane, and learn about their various minifigures, weapons, and vehicles. Meet their first enemies, the terrifying Skeleton Army, and find out everything you ever wanted to know about these bony villains and their vehicles. If you dare, read all about the Ninja's second deadly foe, the Serpentine. Discover the secrets of this sinister snake army and meet all the evil Serpentine minifigures, from the smallest to the tallest.

To find out more about this minifigure see p.38

HOW TO USE THIS BOOK
This book is a comprehensive guide to every LEGO Ninjago minifigure, vehicle, and location released so far. Divided into chapters for each series, the first part of the book examines the 2011 Ninja and their locations, weapons, and dragons. Then we meet the Ninja's enemies, the evil Skeleton Army, and their vehicles. The second part of the book covers the 2012 sets, introducing the newest Ninja minifigures and locations, and their Serpentine enemies. Ninja Files in this section relate to the most recent set that the minifigure has appeared in, although he or she may have featured in more than one set.

The final part of the book has a comprehensive list of all the Ninjago minifigures and sets for all the fact-loving LEGO fans!

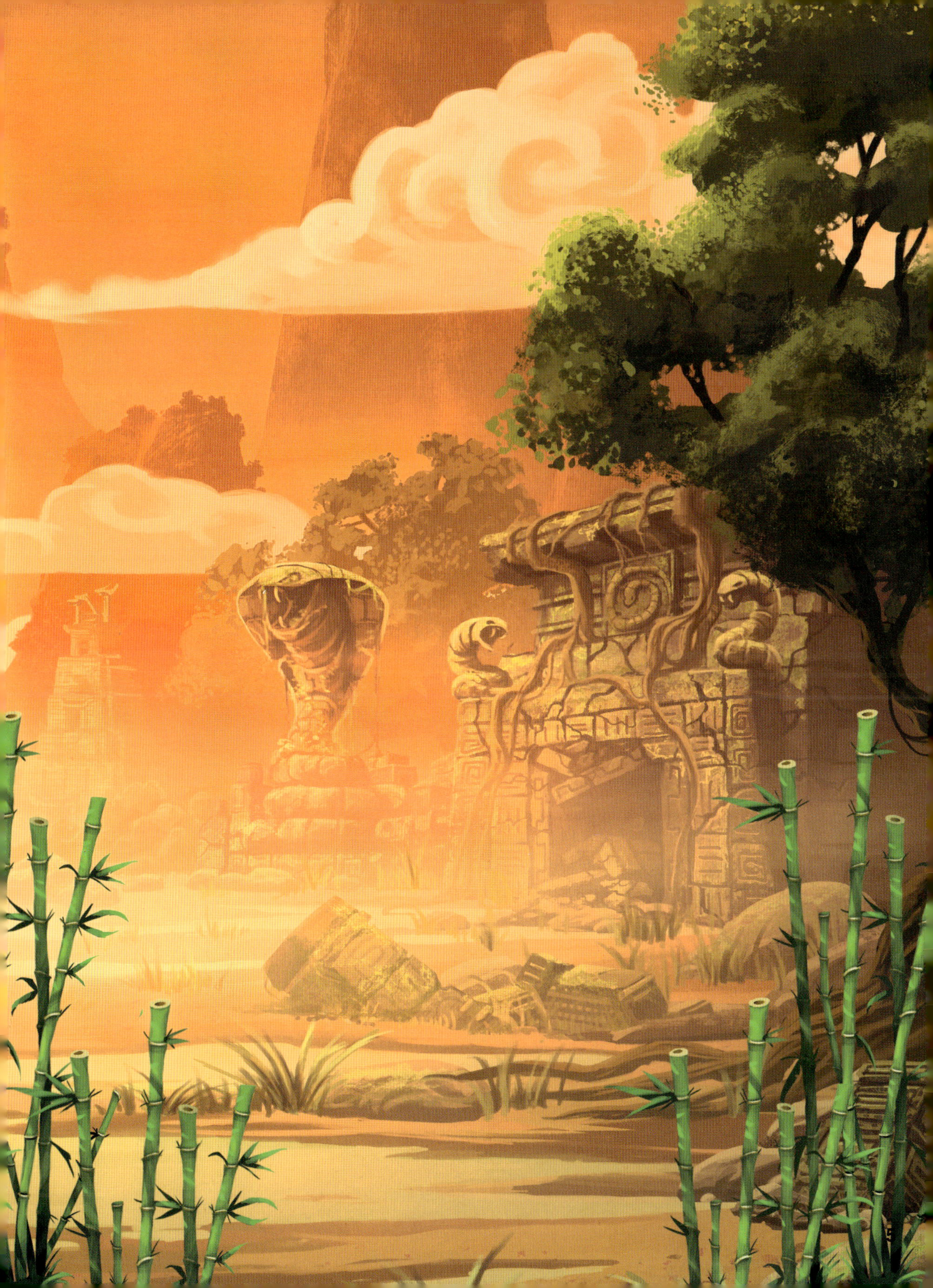

HISTORY OF NINJAGO

A very long time ago, the land of Ninjago was created by the first Master of Spinjitzu, using the four Golden Weapons. Stories tell of the mysterious energy of these Elemental Weapons whose combined power was so great that no single person could handle them all at one time.

The Spinjitzu Master told his two sons—Sensei Wu and Lord Garmadon—about the power of these legendary Weapons. He revealed that if the Weapons ever fell into evil hands, it would lead to chaos and the destruction of Ninjago. The Master said they must be protected at all costs, so when he died his sons swore to keep the Weapons safe.

While Sensei Wu was a good and wise person, his brother Lord Garmadon was evil and wicked. He wanted to possess the Weapons for his own terrifying purposes. The two brothers fought a terrible battle but Sensei Wu emerged victorious. Lord Garmadon was defeated and banished to the Underworld. Sensei Wu then hid the Weapons in the far corners of Ninjago, and peace returned. Until now...

DID YOU KNOW?
There are four Elements of Ninjago—Fire, Ice, Earth, and Lightning. Each Element is linked to a Golden Weapon: the Dragon Sword of Fire (Fire), the Shurikens of Ice (Ice), the Scythe of Quakes (Earth), and the Nunchucks of Lightning (Lightning).

SENSEI WU

Shurikens of Ice

Scythe of Quakes

Nunchucks of Lightning

Dragon Sword of Fire

SECRET MAP
Only Sensei Wu knows where the four Golden Weapons are. He has a map of Ninjago showing their secret locations, but he has hidden that too. He is determined that his brother will not find it!

SPINJITZU
Spinjitzu is an ancient martial art, which allows any Master of it to spin so quickly that he becomes a tornado of energy. Spinjitzu Masters usually control one of the four Elements.

LORD GARMADON

NINJA VS. SKELETON

"I WILL NOT BE DEFEATED BY A PILE OF BONES! NINJA-GO!"

SEASON ONE OF LEGO® Ninjago sees the return of Lord Garmadon. Sensei Wu trains four Ninja to help him defeat his evil brother. However, Garmadon is not alone—he has a mighty Skeleton Army. A total of sixteen awesome LEGO sets bring the season one characters, weapons, vehicles, and locations to life. Turn the page to find out more...

BANZAI! MY ICY POWER WILL SOON QUENCH YOUR FIRE, NINJA!

LORD GARMADON RETURNS

Peace in Ninjago is about to come to an end: Lord Garmadon has returned from the Underworld to search for the four Golden Weapons. And this time he has brought reinforcements—an evil Skeleton Army (also known as Skulkins).

Sensei Wu has a plan. He seeks out four young men—Cole, Jay, Kai, and Zane—whom he can train to become Ninja. These four Ninja will learn to be great warriors, and each will become a master of one of the Elements and a protector of one of the four Golden Weapons.

The Ninja are first put to the test when the Skeletons kidnap Kai's sister, Nya, and steal the map showing the location of the Golden Weapons. The boys put their training into action to rescue Nya and defeat the Skulkins. They also find the Sword of Fire. Further battles follow as the Ninja seek to gain all the Golden Weapons.

In one final attempt to beat his brother, Sensei Wu, Lord Garmadon lures the Ninja to his Dark Fortress. Can the Ninja defeat the mighty Lord Garmadon and his evil Skeleton Army? Turn to p.86 to find out!

FOUR BRAVE BOYS
Sensei Wu wants each of the Ninja to become a Spinjitzu Master of their Elements, so that they can help him prevent his evil brother, Lord Garmadon, from destroying Ninjago.

Jay and the Nunchucks of Lightning

Zane and the Shurikens of Ice

Cole and the Scythe of Quakes

Kai and the Sword of Fire

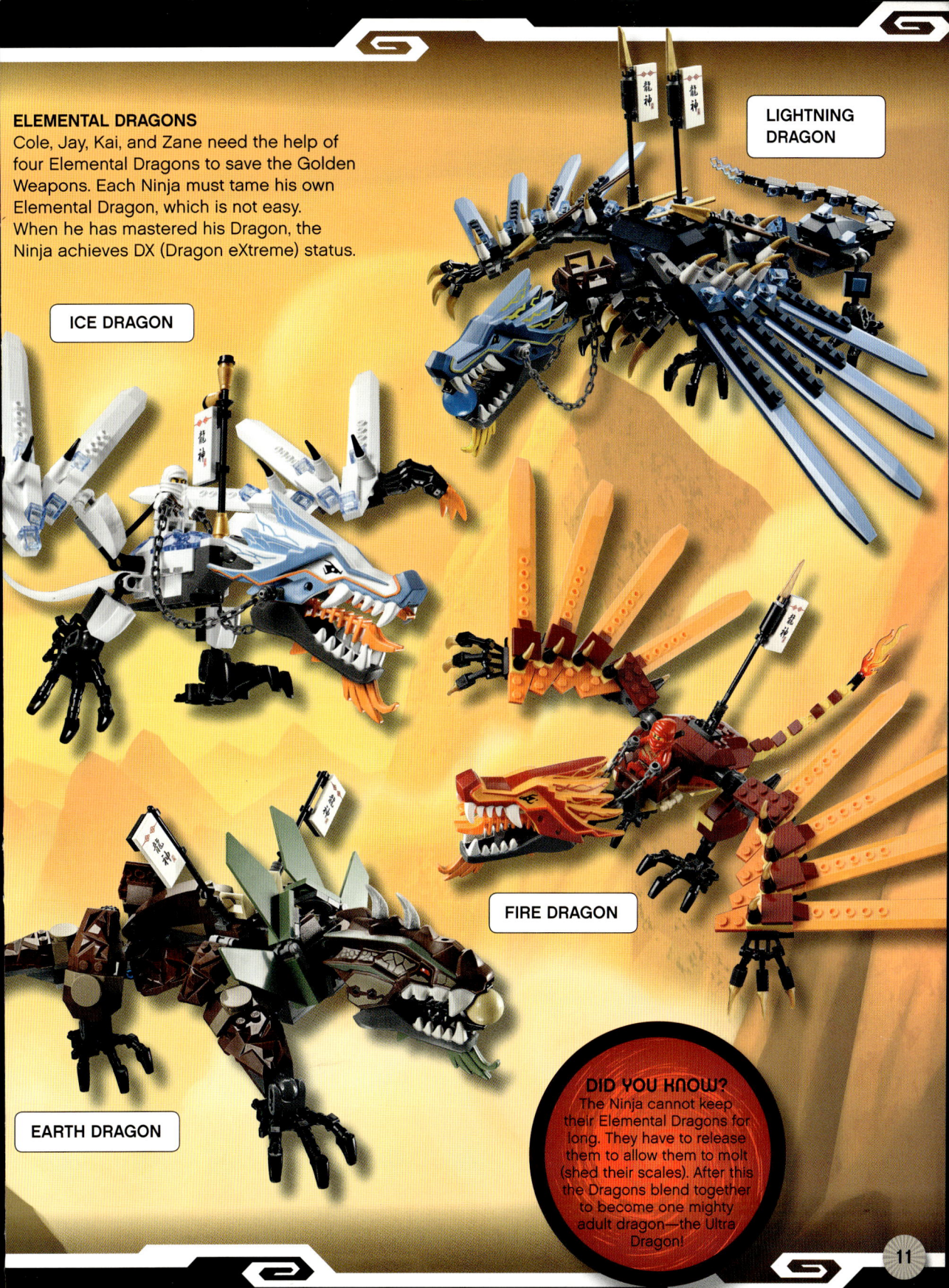

ELEMENTAL DRAGONS

Cole, Jay, Kai, and Zane need the help of four Elemental Dragons to save the Golden Weapons. Each Ninja must tame his own Elemental Dragon, which is not easy. When he has mastered his Dragon, the Ninja achieves DX (Dragon eXtreme) status.

ICE DRAGON

LIGHTNING DRAGON

FIRE DRAGON

EARTH DRAGON

DID YOU KNOW?
The Ninja cannot keep their Elemental Dragons for long. They have to release them to allow them to molt (shed their scales). After this the Dragons blend together to become one mighty adult dragon—the Ultra Dragon!

MEET THE NINJA

SENSEI WU

Wise Sensei Wu knows what it takes to be a great Ninja, so he can see who has potential. He chooses four boys to help him save Ninjago from his brother.

ALL THAT STANDS between Lord Garmadon and the four Golden Weapons is Sensei Wu and his four Ninja. Each individual Ninja is strong and brave, but together they are more than a match for the dark Lord and his Skeleton Army. Sensei Wu has trained them well. Young Nya longs to be a Ninja, like her brother, but she is not ready to join them yet.

KAI

Fire

Before he became a Ninja, Kai was a blacksmith. Now he is the Ninja of Fire!

ZANE

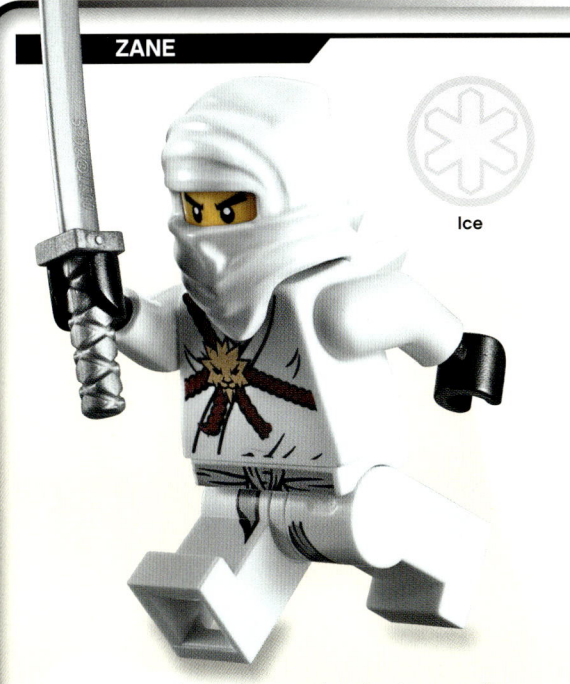

Ice

Ice Ninja Zane looks human but he is actually a robot. His fellow Ninja Jay calls him a "nindroid!"

NYA

Nya is Kai's younger sister. She also used to be a blacksmith, but now she wants to help save Ninjago.

JAY

Lightning

Lightning Ninja Jay is as fast as Lightning, especially when he is doing Spinjitzu!

COLE

Earth

Earth Ninja Cole is the leader of the team, and the strongest. He is not to be messed with!

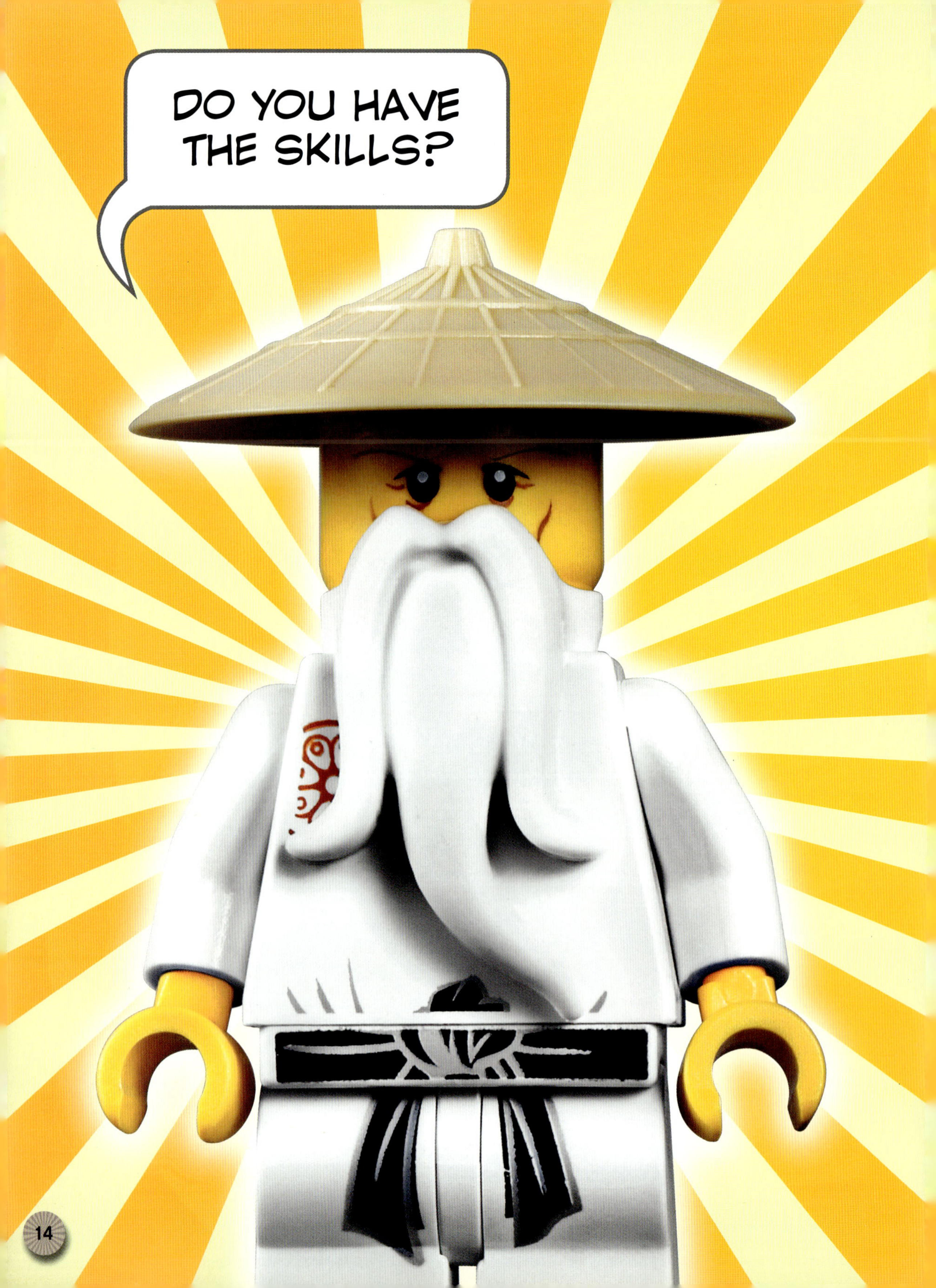
DO YOU HAVE THE SKILLS?

TO BECOME A TRUE NINJA YOU MUST:

FIND AND CONTROL YOUR ELEMENT

ALWAYS BE LOYAL TO YOUR FRIENDS

LEARN TO WIELD MANY TYPES OF WEAPONS

MASTER THE ART OF STEALTH

KAI
NINJA OF FIRE

THIS MINIFIGURE'S Element is Fire and his temper is hot! Kai accepts Sensei Wu's challenge to train as a Ninja, but he must work hard to control his anger and impatience. Sensei Wu's faith in Kai is justified—he becomes a brave, loyal, and skillful Ninja warrior.

Traditional Ninja head wrap made from two scarves tied around the head to leave only the eyes uncovered

Golden badge showing the Fire Element symbol

Sashes and belts are an essential part of a Ninja's outfit.

WEAPONS

BLACK SPEAR
Ninja training consists of 18 disciplines called "ninja juhachi kei." One of these disciplines, "Sojitsu," is all about learning spear techniques.

The two blades slot together.

BLADESTAFF
This double-bladed dagger, or bladestaff, is good for attacking many enemies at once.

GOLDEN KATANA
This weapon is a golden variation of a traditional Ninja sword.

BLACKSMITH
Kai and his sister, Nya, took over the Four Weapons Blacksmith Shop when their father died. There they forged weapons and armor. Sensei Wu saw that Kai had the potential to be more than a blacksmith and planned to use Kai's natural "Fire" and train him to become a Master of Spinjitzu.

NINJA FILE
SET NAME	KAI
SET NUMBER	2111
YEAR	2011
PIECES	19

SPINJITZU

Spinjitzu is an ancient martial art which, once learned, allows the Master to spin fast enough to become a tornado of energy. Kai is training with Sensei Wu to be a Master and become a burning Fire tornado, sizzling with fiery energy.

DID YOU KNOW?
At first Kai did not want to accept Sensei Wu's offer to train to be a Ninja. However, when the Skulkins kidnapped Nya and Wu told him the history of Ninjago, Kai changed his mind. He knew becoming a Ninja would help him to save his sister, and Ninjago.

Kai's Ninja hood is red, like the Element of Fire.

Battle-scarred face with determined expression

Ninja jacket or "uwagi" with sashes and Fire badge

Silver katana

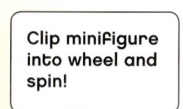

The traditional Ninja belt is called an obi.

Clip minifigure into wheel and spin!

NINJA SKILL

Ninja have to be versatile, adaptable, and disciplined. Their training is intense and pushes them to extremes. A Ninja has to learn how to fight with many different weapons and master many martial arts. Kai uses his speed and grace to help him become a skilled Ninja.

Spinner base

Orange Fire spinner

17

NYA
SISTER OF FIRE

NYA IS KAI'S younger sister. She works with Kai in the Four Weapons Blacksmith Shop. Although she isn't a Ninja, Nya is determined to be better than the boys. She trains hard and, with a veil to mask her identity, she is always ready to battle evil.

NINJA FILE

- SET NAME NYA
- SET NUMBER 2172
- YEAR 2011
- PIECES 21

Red veil to hide her identity

Sleeveless red dress decorated with a phoenix bird pattern

WEAPONS

STAFF
This large wooden pole is a powerful defensive weapon, especially in the hands of a skilled fighter like Nya.

Sharp golden blade

GOLDEN NICK DAGGERS
The golden dagger is seriously sharp and especially effective when used in a pair.

GIRL POWER
Nya is kind and gentle, but also courageous and brave. She is gifted with natural psychic powers. All Nya's special abilities prove very useful when she is battling the evil Skeleton Army.

SECRET SPINNER

Nya hides her true identity so that she can help the Ninja in their fight against evil. With her super secret skills and her orange fire spinner, Nya can spin up a fiery tornado of energy. GO NYA, NINJA-GO!

Nya's hair piece was first used for Irina Spalko in LEGO® Indiana Jones™.

Nya's face with red veil covering her determined expression

Patterned sash ties like a belt around the dress

DID YOU KNOW?
Nya and Lloyd Garmadon are the only two LEGO Ninjago minifigures to have double-sided heads.

SECRET CRUSH

When she is not battling Skeletons or Serpents, Nya wants to spend time with her favorite Ninja—Jay. Blue is Nya's favorite color so naturally Jay is her favorite Ninja!

Phoenix patterned dress printed on legs

Double-sided head—the other side is veiled

Minifigure clips here, ready to spin!

Orange Fire spinner

Nya has trained herself to use many different Ninja weapons, including the sword.

Spinner base

BLACKSMITH SHOP

FAMILY BUSINESS

KAI AND NYA run their father's blacksmith shop, the Four Weapons. Their father was Sensei Wu's most trusted friend, so Wu asked him to draw a map showing the locations of the hiding place of the four Weapons of Spinjitzu. Kai and Nya's father hid the map inside the banner of the shop.

Secret spinning rack

SECRET GEARS
When the roof is lifted it also uncovers a secret gear mechanism, which turns to reveal even more hidden weapons—four Ninja swords!

SECRET WEAPONS
Lift the roof of the shop to reveal a hidden rack on its underside that holds axes, spears, and other weapons and Ninja accessories.

Arsenal of weapons

Roof hinge and gear mechanism

Map shows the location of Golden Weapons

Weapons clip onto the underside of the roof

Golden katana sword on blacksmith's work bench

MINIFIGURES
Kruncha comes to the Four Weapons to steal the Golden Weapons secret location map. Kai has to fight him off using his hidden stash of weapons.

Kruncha

Kai

NINJA FILE

SET NAME	BLACKSMITH SHOP
SET NUMBER	2508
YEAR	2011
PIECES	189

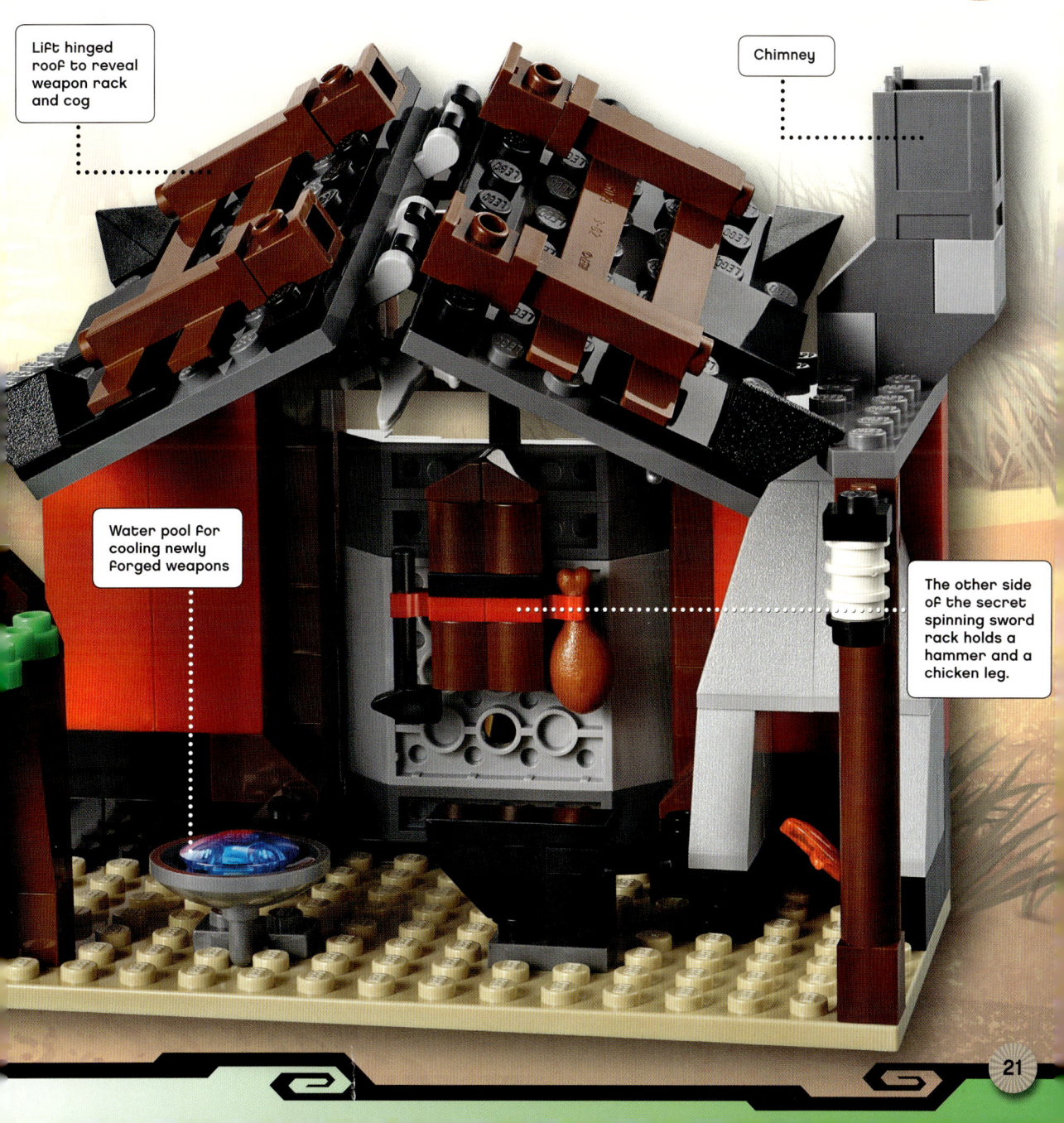

Lift hinged roof to reveal weapon rack and cog

Chimney

Water pool for cooling newly forged weapons

The other side of the secret spinning sword rack holds a hammer and a chicken leg.

SENSEI WU

SPINJITZU MASTER

MASTER OF THE power of creation, Sensei Wu is the son of the first Spinjitzu Master who created Ninjago. He is also the brother of Lord Garmadon. Sensei Wu is strong, wise, and patient. His mission is to protect Ninjago...

Traditional conical hat, often worn by farmers or monks

Sensei Wu's beard and mustache are removable.

Black kimono robe with golden writing to protect Sensei Wu from evil

NINJA FILE

SET NAME	SENSEI WU
SET NUMBER	2255
YEAR	2011
PIECES	20

WEAPONS

STAFF OF THE DRAGONS
Spun quickly, the staff becomes a crushing wall with the strength of a dragon.

Tooth of a golden T-Rex

GOLDEN CHAINED FANG
This chained fang is one of the most valuable weapons in Ninjago.

GOLDEN KATANA
The katana is the most famous, expensive, and prized Japanese sword.

NINJA MASTER
Sensei Wu may be very old, but he is an expert Ninja and a fearless warrior. Wu makes his students train every day, and tells them to use their brains as well as their strength. Without wisdom you can't win

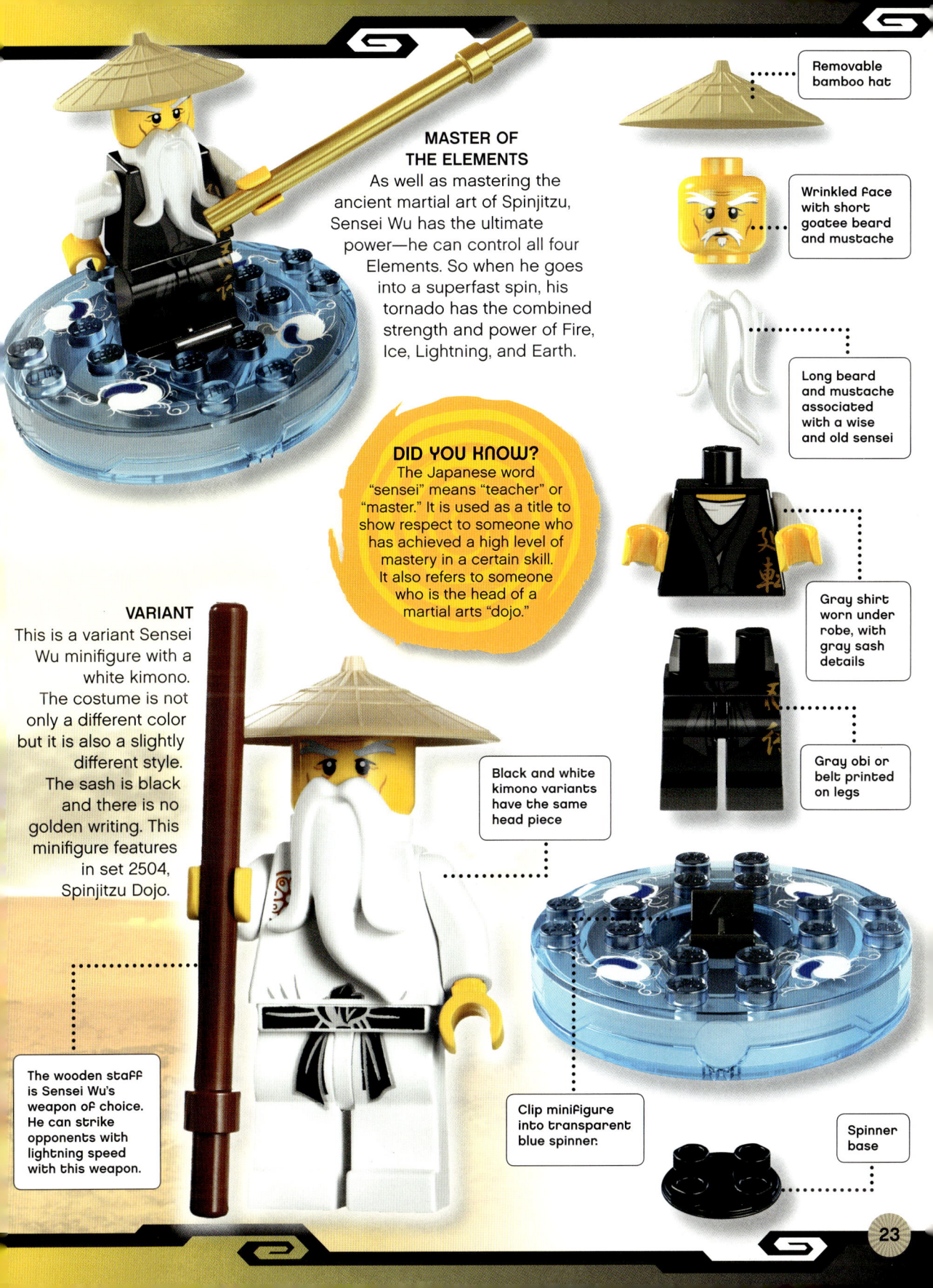

MASTER OF THE ELEMENTS

As well as mastering the ancient martial art of Spinjitzu, Sensei Wu has the ultimate power—he can control all four Elements. So when he goes into a superfast spin, his tornado has the combined strength and power of Fire, Ice, Lightning, and Earth.

Removable bamboo hat

Wrinkled face with short goatee beard and mustache

Long beard and mustache associated with a wise and old sensei

Gray shirt worn under robe, with gray sash details

Gray obi or belt printed on legs

DID YOU KNOW?
The Japanese word "sensei" means "teacher" or "master." It is used as a title to show respect to someone who has achieved a high level of mastery in a certain skill. It also refers to someone who is the head of a martial arts "dojo."

VARIANT
This is a variant Sensei Wu minifigure with a white kimono. The costume is not only a different color but it is also a slightly different style. The sash is black and there is no golden writing. This minifigure features in set 2504, Spinjitzu Dojo.

Black and white kimono variants have the same head piece

Clip minifigure into transparent blue spinner

Spinner base

The wooden staff is Sensei Wu's weapon of choice. He can strike opponents with lightning speed with this weapon.

23

SPINJITZU DOJO

NINJA TRAINING

A DOJO IS a special place where the Ninja go to train. Sensei Wu makes the four Ninja work very hard—they have to dodge falling axes, avoid spinning swords, and swing over snake and fire pits. With practice, these challenges are no problem for the Ninja.

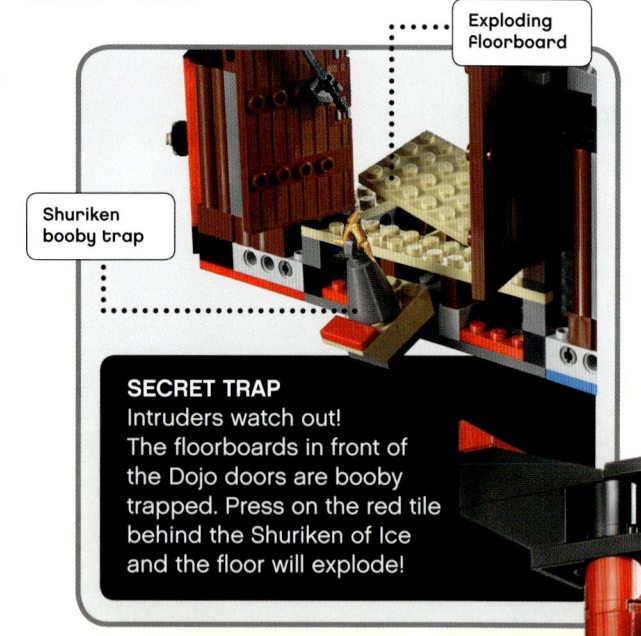

Exploding floorboard

Shuriken booby trap

SECRET TRAP
Intruders watch out! The floorboards in front of the Dojo doors are booby trapped. Press on the red tile behind the Shuriken of Ice and the floor will explode!

Falling axes

NINJA FILE
SET NAME	SPINJITZU DOJO
SET NUMBER	2504
YEAR	2011
PIECES	373

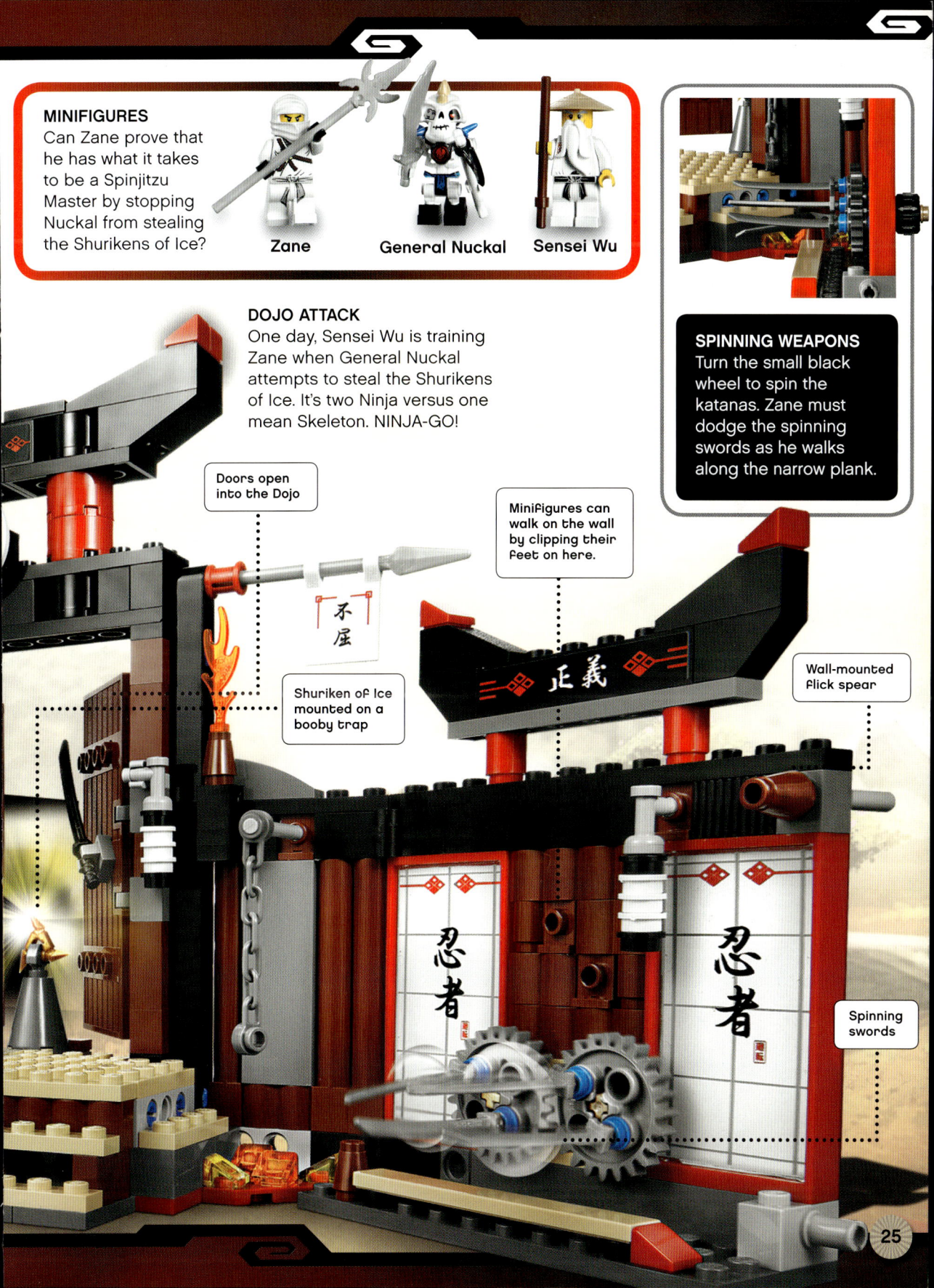

MINIFIGURES
Can Zane prove that he has what it takes to be a Spinjitzu Master by stopping Nuckal from stealing the Shurikens of Ice?

Zane **General Nuckal** **Sensei Wu**

DOJO ATTACK
One day, Sensei Wu is training Zane when General Nuckal attempts to steal the Shurikens of Ice. It's two Ninja versus one mean Skeleton. NINJA-GO!

SPINNING WEAPONS
Turn the small black wheel to spin the katanas. Zane must dodge the spinning swords as he walks along the narrow plank.

Doors open into the Dojo

Minifigures can walk on the wall by clipping their feet on here.

Shuriken of Ice mounted on a booby trap

Wall-mounted flick spear

Spinning swords

25

JAY
NINJA OF LIGHTNING

LIGHTNING IS HIS Element and Jay is lightning-fast in combat. His flair for crazy inventions, his thirst for adventure, and his sense of humor are just some of the qualities that Sensei Wu knew would make him a good skillful Ninja. Jay is also creative and loves solving problems.

NINJA FILE
- **SET NAME** SPINJITZU STARTER SET
- **SET NUMBER** 2257
- **YEAR** 2011
- **PIECES** 57

Traditional Ninja hood in blue, Jay's elemental color

NINJA TRAINING
Jay often uses his sense of humor to distract his enemies in battle, but he always takes his Ninja duties seriously. His lightning speed and agility mean he can easily wield two weapons at once to counter a double attack!

Golden emblem on robe is the symbol for Lightning

The Ninja sash is a good place to hide weapons.

WEAPONS

SILVER KATANA
All Ninja must be able to fight with a sword. The training is tiring and difficult, but Ninja have to learn to persevere. Jay never gives up on anything.

GOLDEN SPEAR
The rarest of the Ninja spears, this golden weapon is extremely sharp and dangerous.

STAFF
Simple but effective, this basic Ninja weapon is useful in one-on-one combat.

Blue Ninja hood to hide identity

Jay is an expert at throwing a spear at lightning speed.

Frowning expression

Lightning emblem worn on robe and secured with brown cords

Obi sash printed on legs

Clip Jay here and spin a tornado of Lightning!

Spinner base

White, Lightning-themed spinner

LIGHTNING STRIKE
Jay is as fast as a bolt of lightning. He can glide through the air, then strike with deadly accuracy. Watch out Skeletons—Jay is coming after you!

DID YOU KNOW?
Jay loves to invent things. One of his best inventions was a dragon roar amplifier. It helped him persuade a dragon to give him a ride to the Underworld to help find Sensei Wu and the stolen Golden Weapons.

LIGHTNING SPINJITZU
Jay was the first of the four Ninja to master the art of Spinjitzu. Now, as quick as a flash, he can spin to turn into a Lightning tornado crackling with electric Ninja energy. However, Jay also has a softer side—he has a secret crush on Kai's sister, Nya.

COLE
NINJA OF EARTH

JUST LIKE EARTH, his Element, Cole is as strong and reliable as a rock. Cole's natural strategic and leadership skills make him a key part of the team. Cole always puts his team first and is a true friend to the other Ninja.

A Ninja wrap provides a good disguise.

Golden emblem showing the Earth symbol.

An obi is a good place to hide weapons.

WEAPONS

BLACK KATANA
To be a skilled swordsman, training is essential. The katana is not an easy weapon to master.

STAFF OF THE DRAGONS
In the hands of a Spinjitzu Master, this Golden Staff will knock the enemy out cold.

HAMMER
This is a good weapon for a fight with a Skeleton!

TEAM FIRST
Cole lacked direction and purpose when he first met Sensei Wu. However, becoming a Ninja has changed him. Now Cole enjoys helping others. A successful mission makes him happy and he always puts his team first, whatever the risks to himself.

NINJA FILE
SET NAME	COLE
SET NUMBER	2112
YEAR	2011
PIECES	19

DID YOU KNOW?
Ninja, medieval Japanese warriors, were organized into clans. You had to be born into the clan to be part of it. Ninja were trained from childhood in the arts of fighting, stealth, and survival. Their job was to carry out secret spy missions.

Black Ninja hood—Cole's elemental color

Distinctive bushy eyebrows

Powerful slicing silver blade

Brown cords keep the golden emblem in place.

Cole is always on the lookout for danger.

Gray obi printed on legs and waist

Clip Cole here to spin a mighty tornado!

Green Earth spinner

Spinner base

EARTH SPINJITZU
Cole is a powerful Ninja. When his strength is combined with his unstoppable Earth tornado, it makes him one mighty Spinjitzu Master. Cole can spin dirt and soil into a huge storm, reducing everything in its path to dust.

LEADERSHIP
Sensei Wu always knew that Cole would make a great leader. Cole leads by example, and takes time to watch the other Ninja train so that he knows their individual strengths and weaknesses. This allows him to plan strategies and to tell his team what to do during a battle.

ZANE
NINJA OF ICE

ZANE IS QUIET, serious, and focused. He learns quickly and is curious about everything. Zane is a seer with the power of sixth sense, and it makes him a particularly stealthy warrior. However, Zane has a forgotten past that sets him apart from the other Ninja.

NINJA FILE
- SET NAME ZANE
- SET NUMBER 2113
- YEAR 2011
- PIECES 19

Zane's Ninja wrap is as icy white as his Element.

Golden emblem to represent Element of Ice

Traditional Ninja sash belt to hold robe in place

WEAPONS

FLAT SPEAR
In the hands of a trained Ninja, the spear is a lethal weapon of deadly accuracy.

SILVER KATANA
This prized sword is a top Ninja weapon.

SHURIKENS OF ICE
One of the four Golden Weapons, these icy throwing stars slice through the air to hit their target with force.

NINJA SKILLS
Zane watches and waits for the right moment to strike! He is so quiet and stealthy that he can creep up on his enemies without being detected. He is dedicated and precise in combat, and ready to tackle any task.

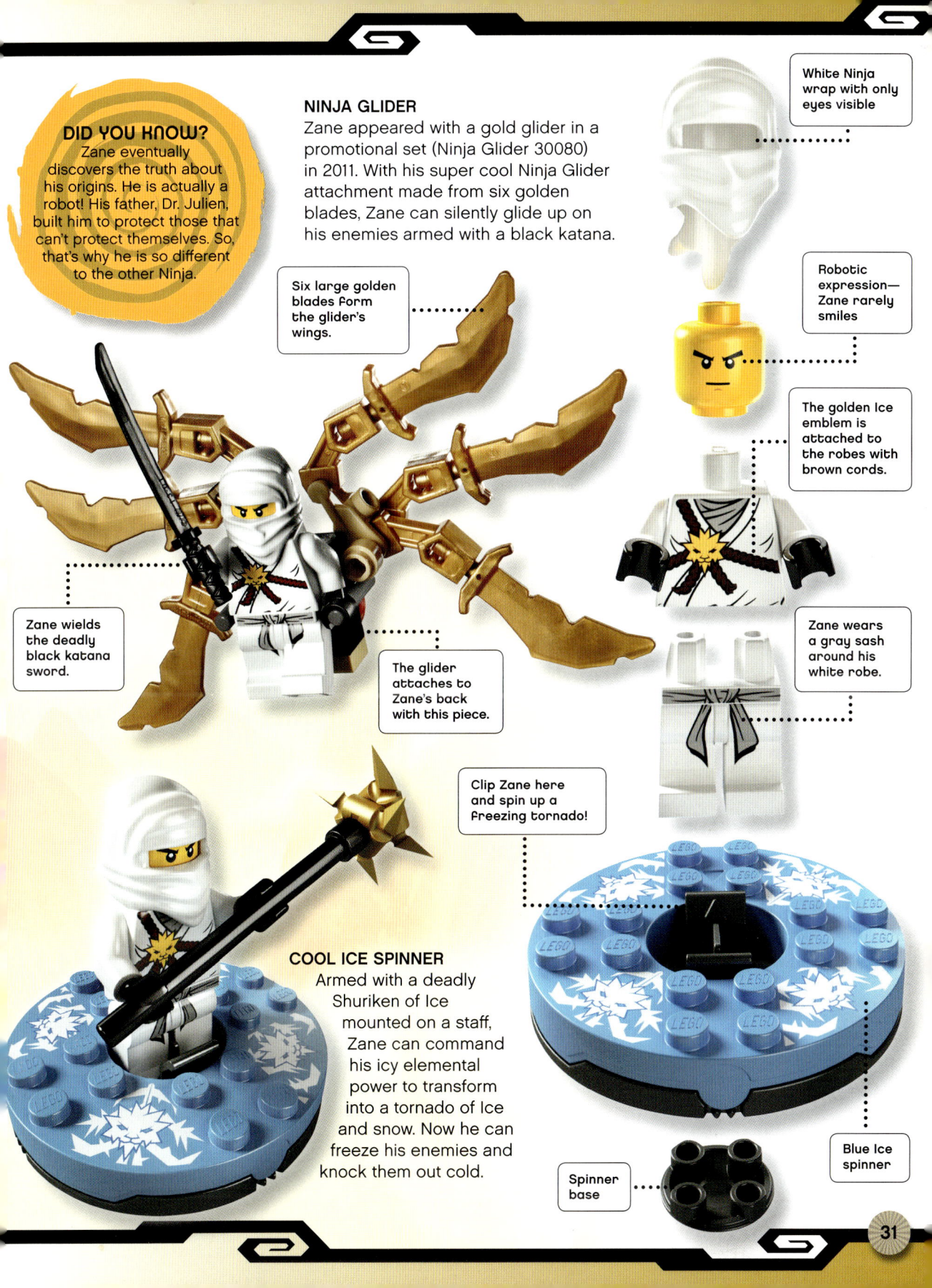

DID YOU KNOW?
Zane eventually discovers the truth about his origins. He is actually a robot! His father, Dr. Julien, built him to protect those that can't protect themselves. So, that's why he is so different to the other Ninja.

NINJA GLIDER
Zane appeared with a gold glider in a promotional set (Ninja Glider 30080) in 2011. With his super cool Ninja Glider attachment made from six golden blades, Zane can silently glide up on his enemies armed with a black katana.

White Ninja wrap with only eyes visible

Six large golden blades form the glider's wings.

Robotic expression— Zane rarely smiles

The golden Ice emblem is attached to the robes with brown cords.

Zane wields the deadly black katana sword.

The glider attaches to Zane's back with this piece.

Zane wears a gray sash around his white robe.

Clip Zane here and spin up a freezing tornado!

COOL ICE SPINNER
Armed with a deadly Shuriken of Ice mounted on a staff, Zane can command his icy elemental power to transform into a tornado of Ice and snow. Now he can freeze his enemies and knock them out cold.

Spinner base

Blue Ice spinner

31

MOUNTAIN SHRINE

SECRET TRAINING GROUND

KAI IS TRAINING hard at the secret Mountain Shrine to increase his Dragon eXtreme (DX) power and master the next level of Spinjitzu. He will need all his skills to protect the Dragon Sword of Fire and his treasure from the evil Skeleton Army.

Sword of Fire can be placed here

Scorpion statue decorates top of shrine

Punching bag can move up and down

Rotate the arch to reveal the treasure chest.

NINJA FILE

SET NAME	MOUNTAIN SHRINE
SET NUMBER	2254
YEAR	2011
PIECES	169

TARGET PRACTICE
The Mountain Shrine set features lots of different weapons and equipment—a double scythe, a chain, a spiked mace ball, and a punching bag. However, Kai's most prized weapon is the rare and precious Golden Dragon Sword!

HIDDEN TREASURE
This set features a treasure chest which can be hidden in the arch underneath the shrine and pulled out when the arch rotates. It also includes a skeleton-style dummy for target practice.

Shrine flame torch

Two gold bars fit inside the treasure chest.

Practice mace ball on ratchet pole that moves up and down

Skeleton dummy

MINIFIGURES
Kai has attained Dragon eXtreme status (see p.38) but he still needs to practice hard to reach the next Ninja level.

Kai DX

Eight spinning ax blades can be attached to the sides of the Shrine.

DID YOU KNOW?
When it is not being used by Kai, the Dragon Sword of Fire can also be clipped between the claws of the scorpion statue on top of the Mountain Shrine.

33

TRAINING OUTPOST

ART OF SPINJITZU

THIS WEAPONS RACK is Cole's portable training outpost. He can set it up anytime and anywhere to practice his Spinjitzu skills. This set comes with five weapons—including two bowie knives—and an archery target.

TARGET PRACTICE
Bullseye! A Ninja needs to have a deadly aim so Kai practices his shooting by firing arrows and throwing the knives at the target. The Skeleton Army had better watch out!

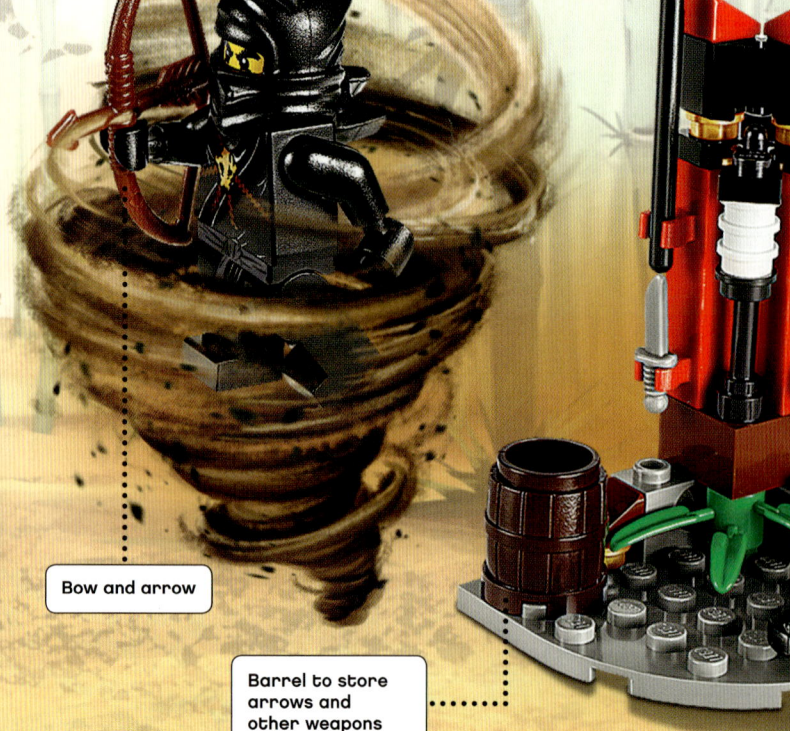

NINJA FILE

SET NAME	NINJA TRAINING OUTPOST
SET NUMBER	2516
YEAR	2011
PIECES	45

Target board

Black spear

Black katana

Bowie knife

Bow and arrow

Barrel to store arrows and other weapons

34

AMBUSH SHRINE

SKELETON ATTACK

SENSEI WU SENDS Kai into a bamboo forest to protect the Scythe of Quakes. But Bonezai wants the weapon too! Kai must hide among the trees and then launch himself at the bony villain. Kai will need his Ninja stealth to beat Bonezai.

NINJA FILE
- **SET NAME** NINJA AMBUSH
- **SET NUMBER** 2258
- **YEAR** 2011
- **PIECES** 71

FLYING ATTACK!
Flick the red LEGO piece down hard to launch the Ninja into the air from his hiding place behind the bamboo trees. NINJA-GO!

- Minifigure launch pad
- Scythe of Quakes
- Bamboo plants move aside when the Ninja is launched!
- Flick here to launch Ninja

Fire Dragon's wings

Green dragon statue

Walls decorated with dragon artwork

Dragon Sword of Fire, surrounded by ceremonial torches

SPECTACULAR SET
The Fire Temple set is made up of five parts—the Fire Dragon, the two pretty side bridges, a front staircase, and the ornate main temple. Best of all, the Dragon can be fully detached from the Fire Temple.

FIRE TEMPLE

SECRET HIDING PLACE

SENSEI WU HAS hidden the Dragon Sword of Fire in the Fire Temple to stop his evil brother getting hold of it. Unfortunately, Lord Garmadon has discovered its location...

MINIFIGURES
This is the largest set in the first season of LEGO Ninjago. It has seven minifigures and includes all four Golden Weapons.

Zane

Sensei Wu

Samukai

Nya

Kai

Kruncha

Garmadon

DRAGON OF FIRE
Pull the Dragon Sword of Fire to open up the Fire Temple. When the Temple is opened it reveals the Fire Dragon's hiding place. Beware any Skeletons who dare to enter...

Garden shrine with gong and drum sticks

Sword of Fire can be pulled here

Fire Dragon can launch balls of fire!

Cherry blossom tree and bridge

NINJA FILE

SET NAME	FIRE TEMPLE
SET NUMBER	2507
YEAR	2011
PIECES	1180

KAI DX

FIRE DRAGON EXTREME

KAI HAS MANAGED to tame his Dragon and has gained DX (Dragon eXtreme) ranking. This status is reflected in his minifigure's new Ninja Dragon costume. Kai received this robe after he had tamed his Dragon and found the Sword of Fire.

NINJA FILE
- **SET NAME** FIRE TEMPLE
- **SET NUMBER** 2507
- **YEAR** 2011
- **PIECES** 1180

DX SPINNER
When a Ninja reaches DX ranking, his minifigure gets a super gold Spinjitzu spinner. Kai's DX spinner shows the Fire Element symbol. He can whip up a fiery tornado, which has the power and strength of a Dragon.

Golden Fire Dragon printed on the robe breathes the Element of Fire

New dark red obi sash

WEAPONS

Blade shoots fire balls

DRAGON SWORD OF FIRE
This powerful weapon can only be held by someone who has mastered Fire.

DRAGON TAMER
Kai was the first of the Ninja to tame his Dragon. The Ninja needed the Dragons to take them to the Underworld to help Sensei Wu. Kai explained to the Dragon what he wanted and the Dragon agreed to help him.

FIRE DRAGON

FIRE GUARDIAN

THIS MIGHTY FIRE Dragon guards the Golden Dragon Sword of Fire, which Sensei Wu hid in the Fire Temple. When Kai tames this Dragon, he is able to control him.

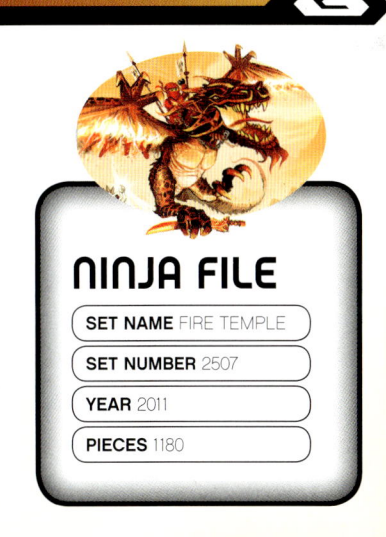

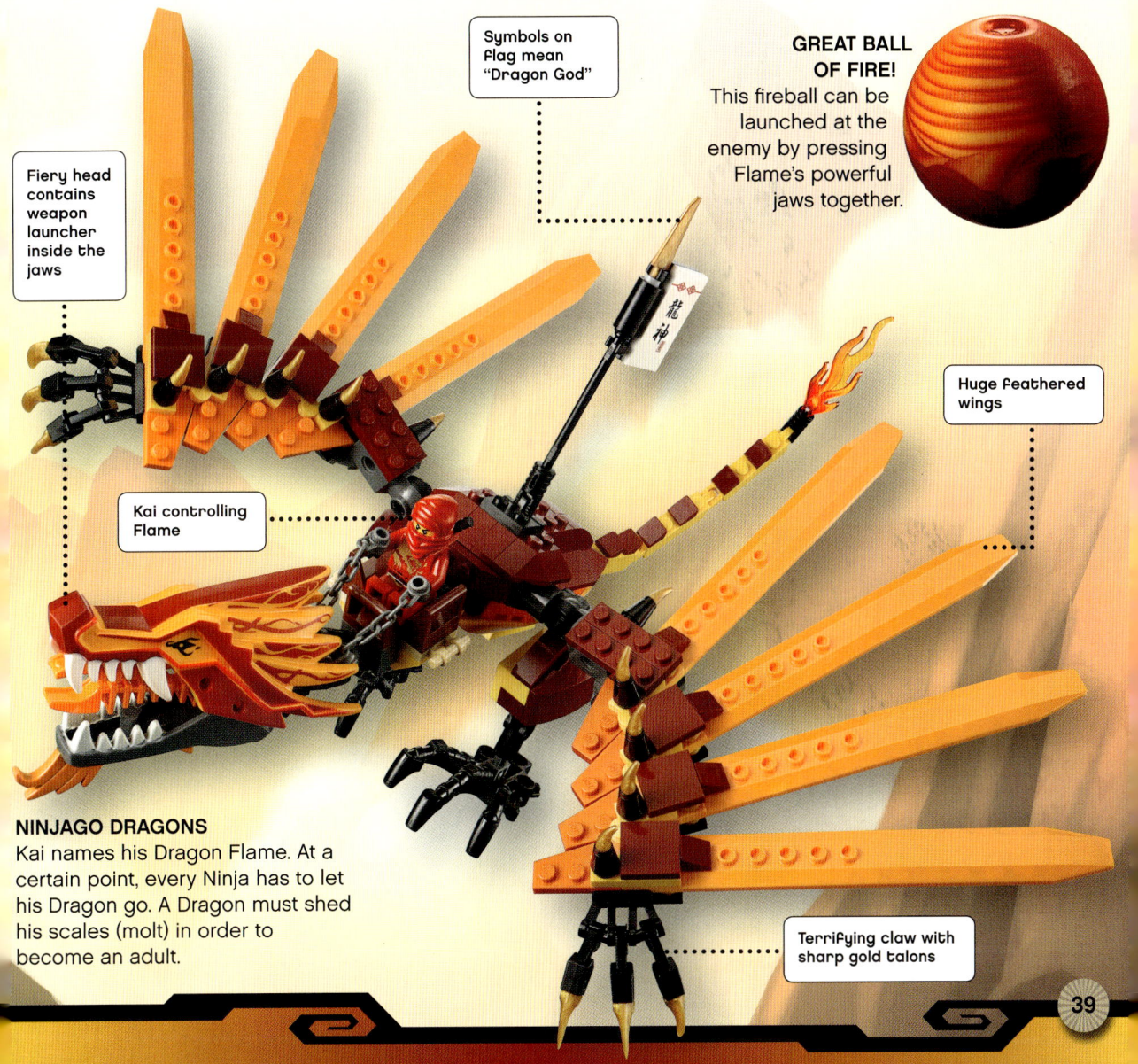

NINJA FILE
- **SET NAME** FIRE TEMPLE
- **SET NUMBER** 2507
- **YEAR** 2011
- **PIECES** 1180

Symbols on flag mean "Dragon God"

GREAT BALL OF FIRE! This fireball can be launched at the enemy by pressing Flame's powerful jaws together.

Fiery head contains weapon launcher inside the jaws

Huge feathered wings

Kai controlling Flame

Terrifying claw with sharp gold talons

NINJAGO DRAGONS
Kai names his Dragon Flame. At a certain point, every Ninja has to let his Dragon go. A Dragon must shed his scales (molt) in order to become an adult.

JAY DX
DRAGON EXTREME

JAY USED HIS inventing skills to tame his Dragon when his jokes and cooking failed to win the Dragon over (see p.27). With his DX Ninja status and the Nunchucks of Lightning, Jay is more than ready to battle against evil.

DX SPINNER
Jay's gold and gray DX spinner shows the Lightning Element symbol. In a flash, Jay spins up a real storm. He is a powerful force of nature ready to battle any enemy.

Golden Lightning Dragon printed on robe is breathing the Element of Lightning

WEAPONS

Curved, slender single-edged blade

BLACK KATANA
After a lot of training and practice, Jay can strike with the speed of lightning using his Ninja sword.

Lightning Dragon detail printed on legs

THE NINJA LIFE
Being a Ninja is not just a job, it is a way of life. Every Ninja has to follow a special code of conduct and commit to the rigorous training and learning of new skills. Jay is a very dedicated Ninja.

NINJA FILE
SET NAME	LIGHTNING DRAGON BATTLE
SET NUMBER	2521
YEAR	2011
PIECES	645

LIGHTNING DRAGON

LIGHTNING GUARDIAN

NINJA FILE

SET NAME LIGHTNING DRAGON BATTLE
SET NUMBER 2521
YEAR 2011
PIECES 645

THIS LIGHTNING DRAGON guards the Golden Nunchucks of Lightning, which Sensei Wu hid in the desolate Floating Ruins. Jay names his Dragon Wisp and once tamed, Wisp is forever loyal to Jay.

Two long spears mounted on the Dragon's wings

Two flags on long spears attached to Dragon's huge body

Deadly flicking tail

BLUE LIGHTNING BALL
Press on the terrifying jaws to launch a lethal Lightning ball at lightning speed!

Lightning ball, ready to be fired!

The Lightning Dragon has four black-clawed feet and two golden-claws on its wings.

MYSTICAL BEASTS
Japanese dragons are known as "tatsu" or "ryu." They are serpent-like and have three-clawed feet. Black dragons symbolize the North; blue the East; white the South, and red the West.

COLE DX
EARTH DRAGON EXTREME

COLE HAS TO overcome his biggest fear—Dragons—to achieve his DX Ninja status. With the courage of a true leader, Cole conquers his fear and learns how to control his Dragon. He becomes very fond of the powerful beast.

NINJA FILE
- **SET NAME** Cole DX
- **SET NUMBER** 2170
- **YEAR** 2011
- **PIECES** 21

WEAPONS

SILVER KATANA
Classic Ninja combat weapon.

BLACK SPEAR
A fast and accurate weapon in the hands of a Ninja.

SCYTHE OF QUAKES
This weapon can cause earthquakes with one mighty blow. It is the ultimate Serpentine repellent.

DRAGON SPINNER
With the newly acquired skills of the Dragon Ninja, Cole can spin up an even bigger tornado. Combined with the power of the Scythe of Quakes, Cole is unstoppable.

Golden Earth Dragon is breathing out the Element of Earth

Earth Dragon's huge scaly tail printed on the legs

DETERMINATION
Cole takes his role as leader of the team very seriously. Now he has reached DX status, he won't rest until he has achieved the next Ninja level.

EARTH DRAGON

EARTH GUARDIAN

NINJA FILE

SET NAME EARTH DRAGON DEFENSE
SET NUMBER 2509
YEAR 2011
PIECES 227

THIS AWESOME EARTH Dragon guards the Scythe of Quakes, which Sensei Wu hid in the Caves of Despair. He is the first of the four Elemental Dragons that the Ninja team encounter in their search for the Golden Weapons. As soon as Cole learns to control the Earth Dragon, he names him Rocky.

STONE MISSILES
Press on the mighty jaws of this huge beast to fire stone ball missiles. The enemy will be falling like boulders!

Swing its tail to catapult boulders at the enemy

Two flags reading "Dragon God" fit onto scaly body

A stone ball missile sits in the Dragon's mouth, ready to be fired.

The Dragon has four huge three-clawed feet.

The Earth Dragon's head is made from a different mold to the other three Dragons.

ARMORED BEAST
Rocky is different to the other three Elemental Dragons—he has spikes on his body, four legs, no arms, smaller armored wings, a different shaped head, and a swinging tail that can launch boulders.

ZANE DX

ICE DRAGON EXTREME

ZANE'S FIRST MEETING with his Dragon didn't go very well—the beast froze Zane into a solid block of ice! As soon as he had thawed out, Zane was able to tame the Dragon and earn his DX (Dragon eXtreme) Ninja status.

Removable hood

NINJA FILE

SET NAME	ZANE DX
SET NUMBER	2171
YEAR	2011
PIECES	22

WEAPONS

NINJAGO SWORD
Zane can wield this Ninja sword with great skill.

FLAIL OF ICE
This golden weapon has the power of solid Ice.

SILVER SPEAR
This weapon can be thrown at enemies.

DRAGON SPINNER
As a DX Ninja, Zane has reached a higher level of Spinjitzu ability and can spin up a terrifying tornado of Ice and snow. Skulkins had better watch out!

Golden Ice Dragon breathes out the Element of Ice

Unique DX printing on torso and legs also continues on back of minifigure

ICE ATTACK!
Now that Zane is a Dragon Ninja, he plans to crush the Skeleton Army with a freezing Ice attack. With the help of his Dragon, Zane will be unstoppable!

ICE DRAGON

ICE GUARDIAN

THIS ICE DRAGON guards the Golden Shurikens of Ice, which Sensei Wu hid inside the Ice Fortress in the Frozen Wasteland. Zane uses his elemental powers to find a cool connection with the mythical beast. He tames the Dragon and names him Shard.

FROZEN BALLS OF ICE
Solid frozen Ice balls can be fired at speed from this icy beast's terrifying jaws.

Zane rides his Dragon from a seat on its back.

Ice feathered wings are movable

Terrifying orange claws

FROZEN BREATH
The Ice Dragon may be the smallest of the Elemental Dragons, but he is just as terrifying as the others. Icy breath shoots out from his jaws, freezing everything in its path.

Ice balls can be fired from the Dragon's jaws.

NINJA FILE

SET NAME	ICE DRAGON ATTACK
SET NUMBER	2260
YEAR	2011
PIECES	158

MEET THE SKELETON ARMY

LORD GARMADON

Lord Garmadon controls the Skeleton Army and it carries out his evil bidding.

THE SKELETON ARMY is a scary sight to behold! These bony bad guys, also known as Skulkins, have come from the Underworld to create trouble in Ninjago. There are four Skulkin Generals and four soldiers. Some of the Skeletons are a little stupid and some are very smart, but all of them are determined to fight the Ninja!

SAMUKAI

Leader of the Skulkins and General of Fire, Samukai is often frustrated by the stupidity of his troops.

KRUNCHA

General Kruncha is Samukai's second-in-command. This fearsome Skulkin is famous for his strength.

46

WYPLASH

General Wyplash is one of the smartest Skeletons. He is good at thinking up nasty plans to thwart the Ninja.

NUCKAL

General Nuckal is very stupid. His contributions to the army include getting into trouble and irritating Kruncha.

BONEZAI

Bonezai is chief designer of all the Skeleton Army's vehicles, including helicopters, motorbikes, and trucks.

KRAZI

Don't be fooled by this wacky warrior, he's no joker. Krazi's speed on the battlefield is legendary.

FRAKJAW

Part of the attack unit, Frakjaw terrifies his enemies with his spiky weapon, also known as a silver battle mace.

CHOPOV

Chopov is famous for his defensive skills. The bony Skulkin also acts as the Skeleton Army's vehicle mechanic.

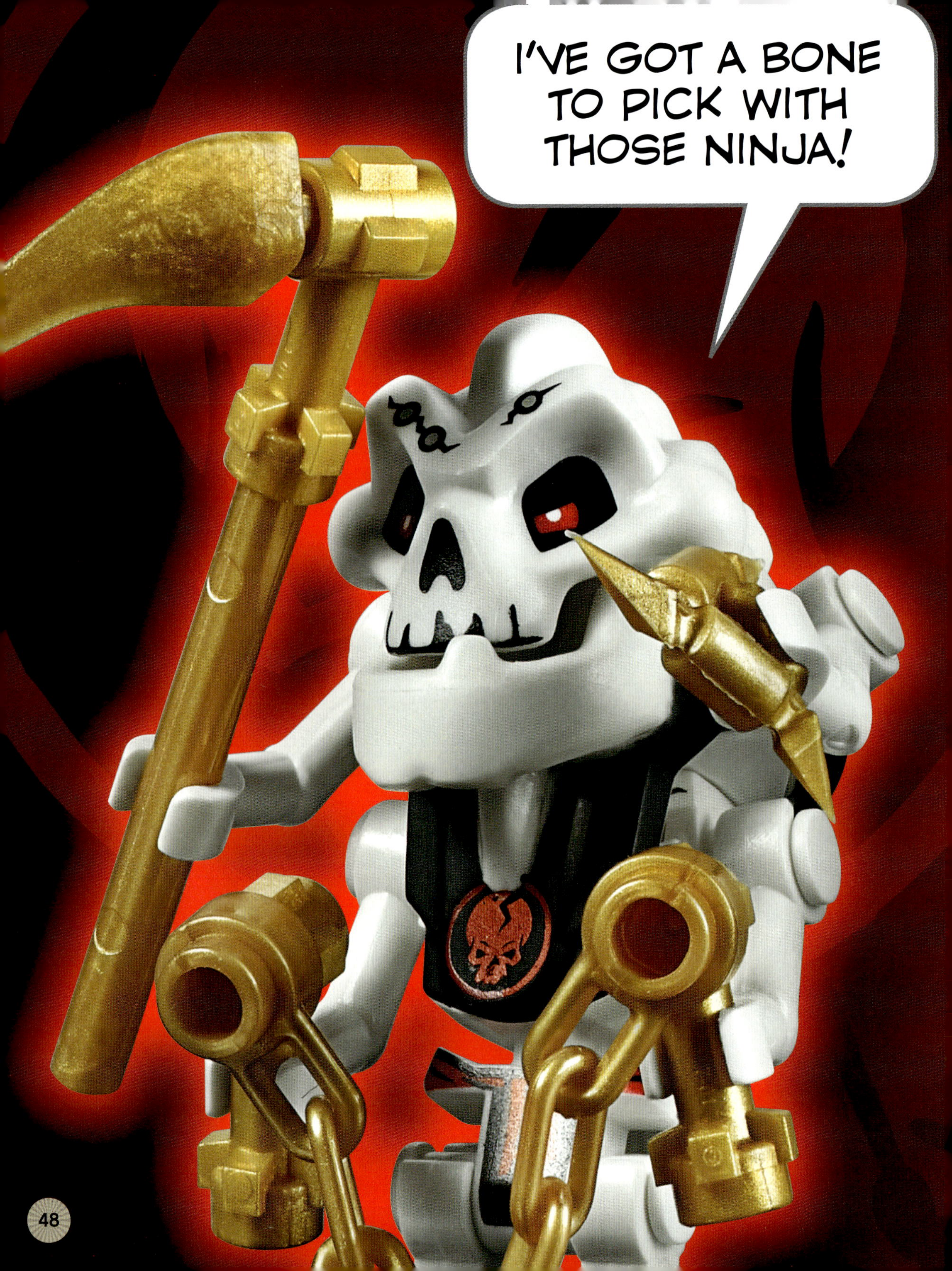
I'VE GOT A BONE TO PICK WITH THOSE NINJA!

THE BACKBONE OF THE SKELETON ARMY IS:

OBEDIENCE

ANGER

RUTHLESSNESS

STUPIDITY

LORD GARMADON
MASTER OF DESTRUCTION

SENSEI WU'S EVIL brother Lord Garmadon is King of the Underworld. With the help of his Skeleton Army, he continues to spread fear on his dark quest to defeat his brother and the Ninja, and to destroy Ninjago.

NINJA FILE
- **SET NAME** Lord Garmadon
- **SET NUMBER** 2256
- **YEAR** 2011
- **PIECES** 23

- Silver samurai helmet originally belonged to Samukai
- Bone attachment to show his status as overlord of the Skeleton Army
- Red eyes and evil grimace
- Visible skeletal ribcage
- Purple obi—Garmadon still wears his Ninja belt

WEAPONS

DOUBLE-BONED SKELI-SCYTHE
A two-headed slicing weapon—double the trouble.

- Bone spear heads
- Lightning-shaped blades

SILVER DARK BLADE
A short sword with a curved blade that fits easily into the folds of the Ninja obi.

THUNDER BOLT
This awesome weapon harnesses the power of Lightning.

THE GREAT DEVOURE
Lord Garmadon wasn' always evil. As a child he was bitten by the snake known as the Great Devourer, and it venom made him turn to the dark side.

SAMUKAI
GENERAL OF FIRE

ONCE THE KING of the Underworld, the fearsome Samukai now leads the Skeleton Army in their battle against the Ninja. Will his hunt for the four Weapons of Spinjitzu be the end of him?

Unique skull markings

Wide, open mouth, unique in LEGO Ninjago minifigures

Four bony arms allow him to wield four weapons at once.

Red skull is the emblem of the Skeleton Army

WEAPONS

SCYTHE OF QUAKES
One of the four mystical Weapons of Spinjitzu.

NUNCHUCKS OF LIGHTNING
Weapon of Spinjitzu powered by a bolt of lightning.

RARE BONES
Samukai is the rarest minifigure in the 2011 LEGO Ninjago range as he only appears in two sets. He is also one of the only three LEGO Ninjago minifigures that don't have spinners.

NINJA FILE

SET NAME	Garmadon's Dark Fortress/Fire Temple
SET NUMBER	2505/2507
YEAR	2011
PIECES	518/1180

FRAKJAW

SKELETON OF FIRE

THIS SCARY RED Skeleton is the toughest Skulkin in Lord Garmadon's Army. He is fiery and angry and loves to fight—especially with Ninja!

NINJA FILE

- **SET NAME** SPINJITZU STARTER SET
- **SET NUMBER** 2257
- **YEAR** 2011
- **PIECES** 57

WEAPONS

GOLDEN BATTLE MACE
This golden ball and chain weapon can be deadly.

BONE
Skeletons love to hit their enemies with a long bone!

DARK BLADE
Only the most destructive Skeletons use this brutal weapon.

- Body armor includes red shoulder pads
- Protective chest plate armor
- Skeleton Army emblem
- Red combat sash

SKELETON WEAPONS

The Skeletons have a terrifying collection of weapons to use in battle. The Ninja need all their skills to defeat this evil enemy. They are brutal and vicious fighters, and the legendary Frakjaw is one of the worst of all.

EVIL FIRE SPINNER
Frakjaw whirls his golden battle mace to spin up a terrible fiery tornado. He leaves a trail of ash and destruction.

Unique Skeleton face

Removable body armor

Traditional bamboo hat

Sash printed on body part

LOUDMOUTH
Frakjaw loves the sound of his own voice and sometimes it is difficult to get him to shut up. He especially likes to taunt and challenge his enemies.

Clip minifigure in place, ready to spin.

53

TURBO SHREDDER

BATTLE FOR THE GOLDEN SCYTHE

FRAKJAW DRIVES THIS terrifying Turbo Shredder. This Skeleton tank has a scary skull at the front, fixed between two large caterpillar track treads. The frightening jaws of the skull snap open and closed as the treads move forward, crushing everything in its path… including Ninja!

DID YOU KNOW?
Frakjaw's name is a play on the words "fracture" (a crack or break in a bone) and "jaw"—a suitably sinister combination for this bony evil villain!

NINJA FILE
SET NAME	TURBO SHREDDER
SET NUMBER	2263
YEAR	2011
PIECES	223

All-terrain rubber treads

MINIFIGURES
Jay and Cole have to use all their Spinjitzu expertise to avoid being swallowed up by the fang-filled jaws of Frakjaw's Turbo Shredder.

Jay   Cole   Frakjaw

GOLDEN SCYTHE MISSION
Frakjaw has stolen the golden Scythe of Quakes. It is Jay and Cole's mission to get it back before Frakjaw hands it over to the evil Lord Garmadon himself. There's only one problem… Frakjaw is escaping in his fearsome tank. Can the Ninja stop him in time and avoid the tank's terrible fangs?

Flames stream from the Turbo Shredder's tail pipes!

Powerful engine sits behind the cockpit

Stolen Scythe of Quakes

Bone embellishments decorate the tank.

Moving, snapping skull's head

Wheels inside the tread roll the machine forward.

SNAP ATTACK
Push the Shredder forward on its tire treads. The forward motion pulls upon a lever mechanism that causes the skull's head to move up and down. Watch out for that snapping jaw!

55

KRAZI
SKELETON OF LIGHTNING

KRAZI BY NAME and crazy by nature, this wild menace is a Skulkin warrior in Lord Garmadon's Skeleton Army. Krazi is the fastest of the Skeletons—when he strikes he is lightning quick. Watch out, he is mad and destructive!

NINJA FILE
- **SET NAME** KRAZI
- **SET NUMBER** 2116
- **YEAR** 2011
- **PIECES** 22

WEAPONS

PICKAX
This grim tool is a lethal weapon in the hands (or bones!) of a crazy Skeleton!

DOUBLE-BLADED BONE DAGGER
Twice as dangerous, this double-bladed dark weapon is truly evil. Ninja beware!

GOLDEN BONE
This hard-hitting weapon is simple but effective. Made of gold, it lasts forever!

- Evil red eyes and crazy red face paint
- Blue shoulder pads are part of body armor
- Protective chest plate armor
- Standard-issue Skeleton Army emblem

BONE TERROR
Dangerous and fearless, Krazi is so crazy that he will pick a fight with anyone. He will try to flatten them with his favorite weapon— a large golden bone!

DID YOU KNOW?
Krazi minifigures feature either a red and blue jester's hat or blue armor, never both. In set 2116, Krazi wears the blue armor.

BLACK LIGHTNING SPINNER
It isn't only Ninja that are mastering the art of Spinjitzu. Some of the villains can also spin up a tornado. Krazi's Lightning tornado is terrifying and fast!

Unique Skeleton face

Removable body armor

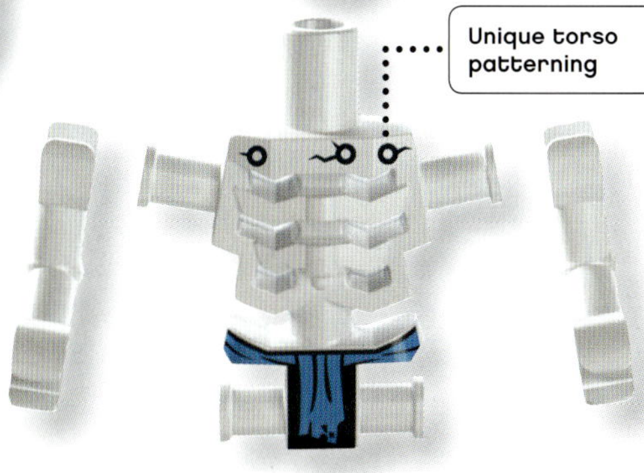

Unique torso patterning

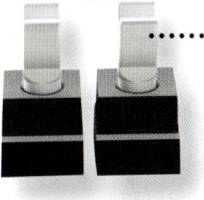

Removable jester's hat

Bone legs with big black boots

Skeleton torso, without armor

Minifigure clips into center of wheel

CRAZY JESTER'S HAT
Krazi's red and blue jester's hat and red face paint are symbols of his craziness. They complete his "mad" look.

Stolen Golden Shuriken of Ice

Spinner base

57

CHOPOV
SKELETON OF EARTH

CHOPOV IS AS tough as a rock. This smart warrior is also the chief mechanic of the Skeleton Army and maintains all of the vehicles. Chopov doesn't let anything get in his way, even Ninja! Beware of his mighty strength.

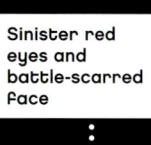

Sinister red eyes and battle-scarred face

NINJA FILE
- **SET NAME** CHOPOV
- **SET NUMBER** 2114
- **YEAR** 2011
- **PIECES** 20

Protective chest plate armor

Emblem strikes fear into enemies' hearts

Black and gray Ninja-like sash

WEAPONS

GOLDEN DARK BLADE
This golden dark blade is a prized and lethal Skeleton weapon and sister weapon to the dark blade.

BONE
No Skeleton warrior should be without a long striking bone.

STAFF
This battle weapon is effective in the hands of a tough Skulkin!

SKELETON MENACE
Chopov's weapon of choice is the dark blade, but he is skilled with many other weapons, including the bone ax. He secretly wishes that he, instead of Bonezai, could design the Skeleton Army's super cool vehicles.

58

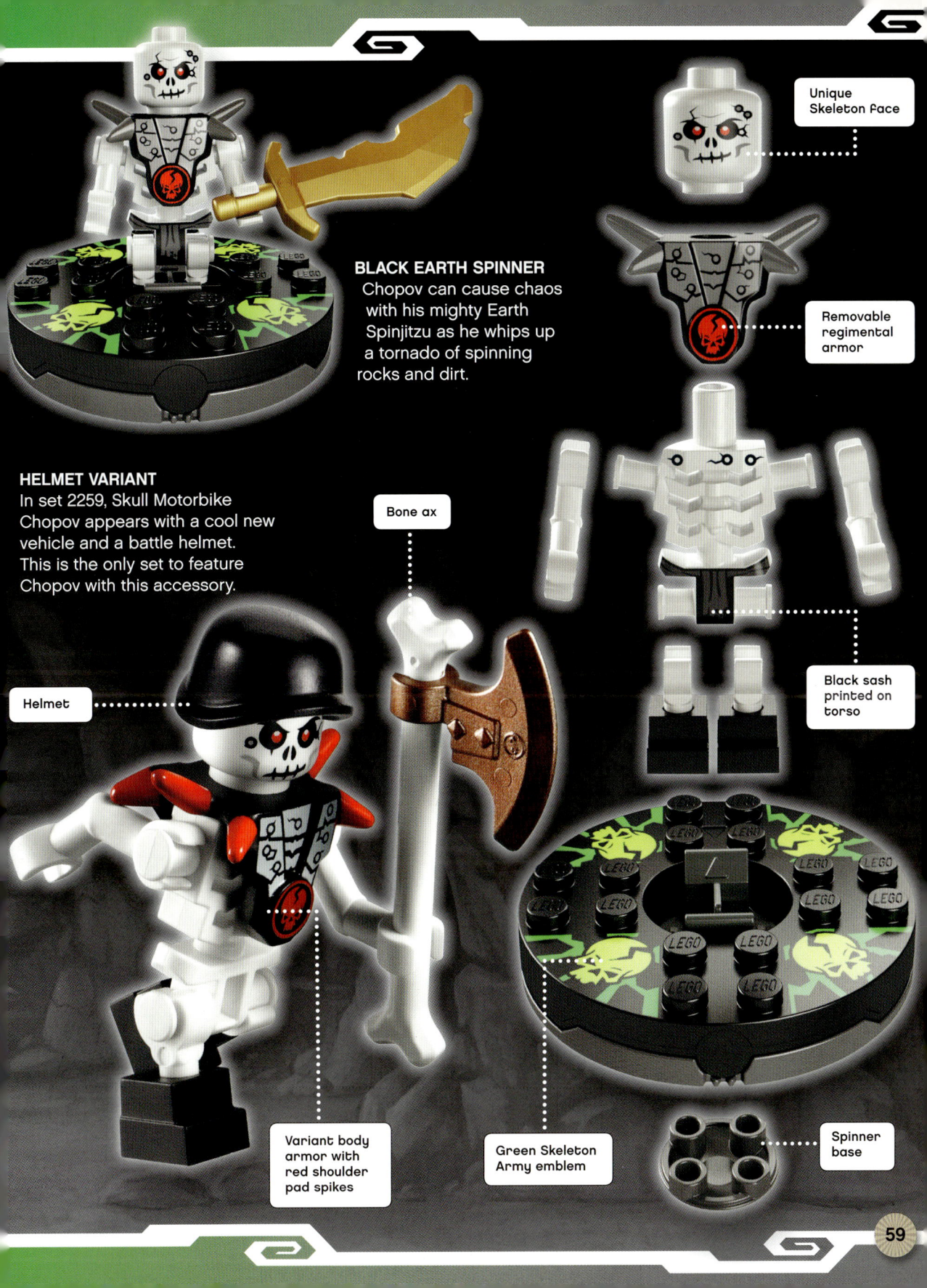

BLACK EARTH SPINNER
Chopov can cause chaos with his mighty Earth Spinjitzu as he whips up a tornado of spinning rocks and dirt.

Unique Skeleton face

Removable regimental armor

Black sash printed on torso

HELMET VARIANT
In set 2259, Skull Motorbike Chopov appears with a cool new vehicle and a battle helmet. This is the only set to feature Chopov with this accessory.

Helmet

Bone ax

Variant body armor with red shoulder pad spikes

Green Skeleton Army emblem

Spinner base

59

SKULL MOTORBIKE

NINJA SWAT DEVICE

CHOPOV'S MENACING battle vehicle is a cool chopper motorbike. He uses it in battle or for quick escapes. The powerful skull hammerhead can smash anything in its path, especially Ninja warriors!

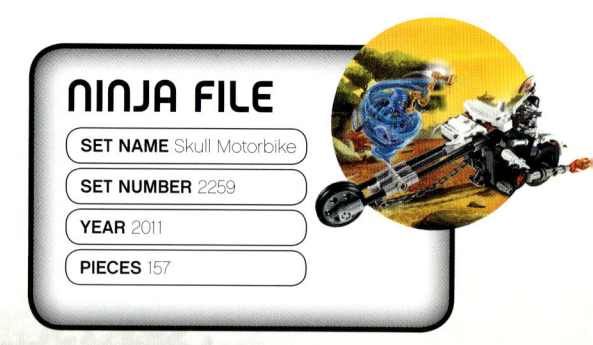

NINJA FILE
- **SET NAME** Skull Motorbike
- **SET NUMBER** 2259
- **YEAR** 2011
- **PIECES** 157

Jay

Chopov

MINIFIGURES
Jay battles with Chopov to stop him escaping with the Nunchucks of Lightning. Can he use his Ninja skills to avoid the skull hammerhead?

Double-tired front wheel to keep motorbike stable

Catapult hinge mechanism

BONE CHROME
The Skull Motorbike is equipped with clever bone features: levers, brakes, and horned spikes for knocking over and spearing the enemy. It is an awesome battle vehicle fit for the Skeleton Army.

DID YOU KNOW?
Although Chopov is a loyal member of the Skeleton Army, he secretly hopes that Bonezai will one day be captured in battle so that he can replace him as the vehicle designer.

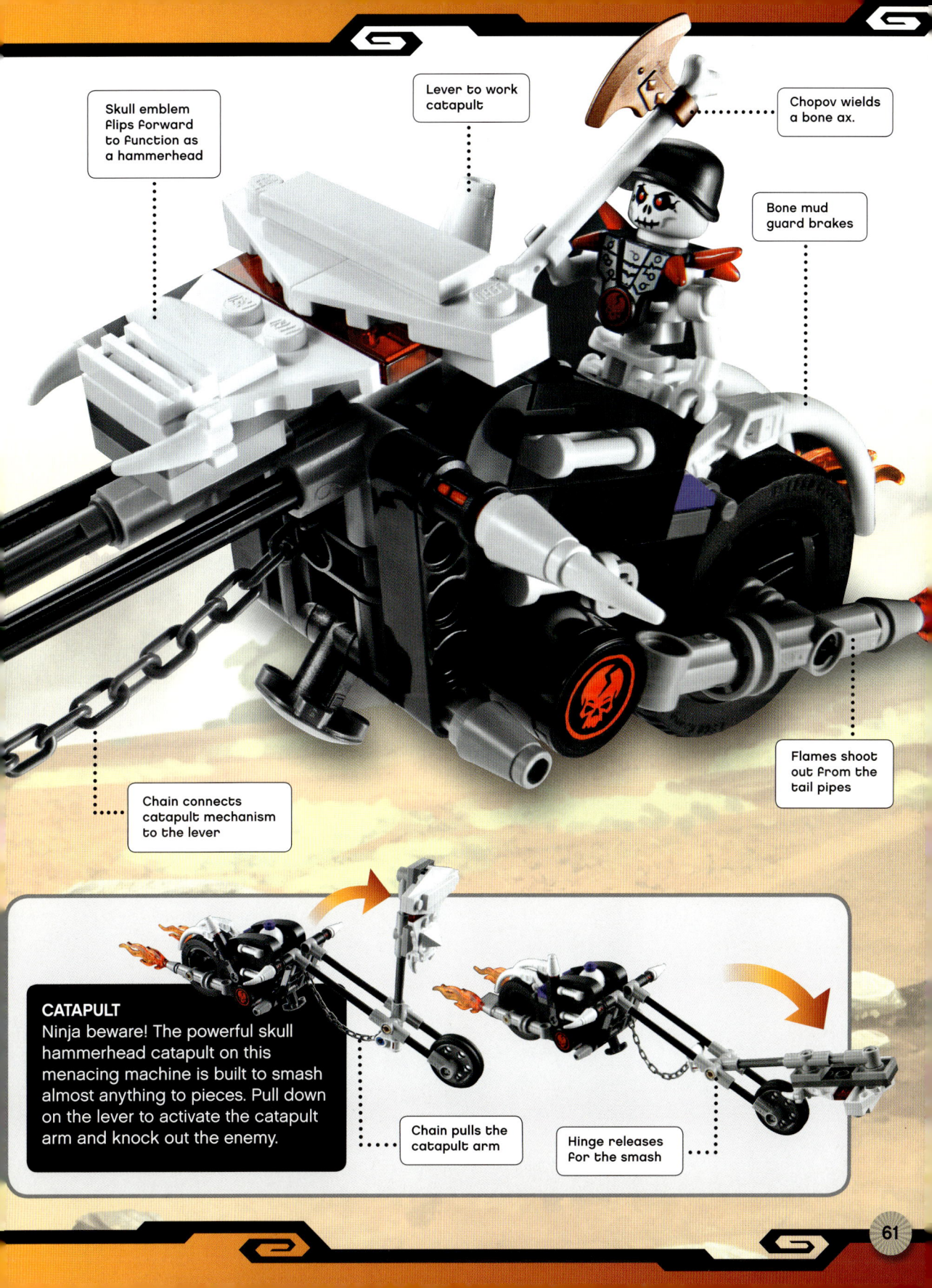

Skull emblem flips forward to function as a hammerhead

Lever to work catapult

Chopov wields a bone ax.

Bone mud guard brakes

Flames shoot out from the tail pipes

Chain connects catapult mechanism to the lever

CATAPULT
Ninja beware! The powerful skull hammerhead catapult on this menacing machine is built to smash almost anything to pieces. Pull down on the lever to activate the catapult arm and knock out the enemy.

Chain pulls the catapult arm

Hinge releases for the smash

BONEZAI

SKELETON OF ICE

BONEZAI DESIGNS ALL the vehicles in the Skeleton Army. This stealthy warrior is as cold as Ice and strikes a chill into the heart of his enemies. Bonezai uses his Ice Element abilities to win weapons and battle for glory.

NINJA FILE

- **SET NAME** BONEZAI
- **SET NUMBER** 2115
- **YEAR** 2011
- **PIECES** 21

WEAPONS

GOLDEN PICKAX
Made from solid gold, every warrior wants this hard-hitting weapon.

SILVER BONE AX
With its super cutting action, this weapon is lethal in the bony hands of an angry Skeleton!

SILVER BATTLE MACE
Big, heavy, and made of solid silver, this swinging weapon can do some serious damage.

- Shoulder spikes can be rammed into opponents in battle
- Protective body armor protects bony rib cage
- Combat sash that Skeleton Army have adopted as part of their uniform

BATTLE CRY!
Bonezai's name is a combination of the Japanese battle cry "banzai" and the word "bone." He is so cold he can even freeze shadows. Watch out for this cool customer, Ninja!

FREEZING ICE SPINNER
When Bonezai spins up a chilling Ice tornado it freezes everything to the bone. Brrrrrrr!

Unique face with red crossed eyes

Detachable body armor with Skeleton Army emblem

STEALTHY SKELETON
Bonezai is strong, brutal, and stealthy. These warrior qualities make him fearsome in battle, especially when he is wielding his weapon of choice—a huge bone ax.

Detachable bone arms

Battle-scarred face

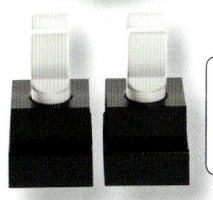

Standard Skeleton torso with sash and body markings

Bone ax with large metal chopping blade

Pale blue Skeleton Army emblem printed on spinner

Spinner base

63

NINJA BATTLE
ARENA

SPIN TO VICTORY!

THIS LIMITED EDITION set is the ultimate test of good versus evil. Earth Ninja Cole must battle the Ice-cold Bonezai for control of the precious Golden Weapons. Spin the minifigures for an epic battle!

Part of the arena wall is decorated like a dojo for the heroic Spinjitzu Ninja.

Place minifigures on their spinners and spin up a super battle tornado.

ENTER HERE! Enemy warriors have separate entrances into the Battle Arena. The Ninja enter through a pagoda-style gateway, while the terrifying Skeletons come in through a bone arch.

Weapons clip on to the wall around the Battle Arena

Scythe

Bone dagger

Spear

Black pinch and fire weapon shoots red ball missiles at the enemy

NINJA FILE
SET NAME	NINJAGO BATTLE ARENA
SET NUMBER	2520
YEAR	2011
PIECES	463

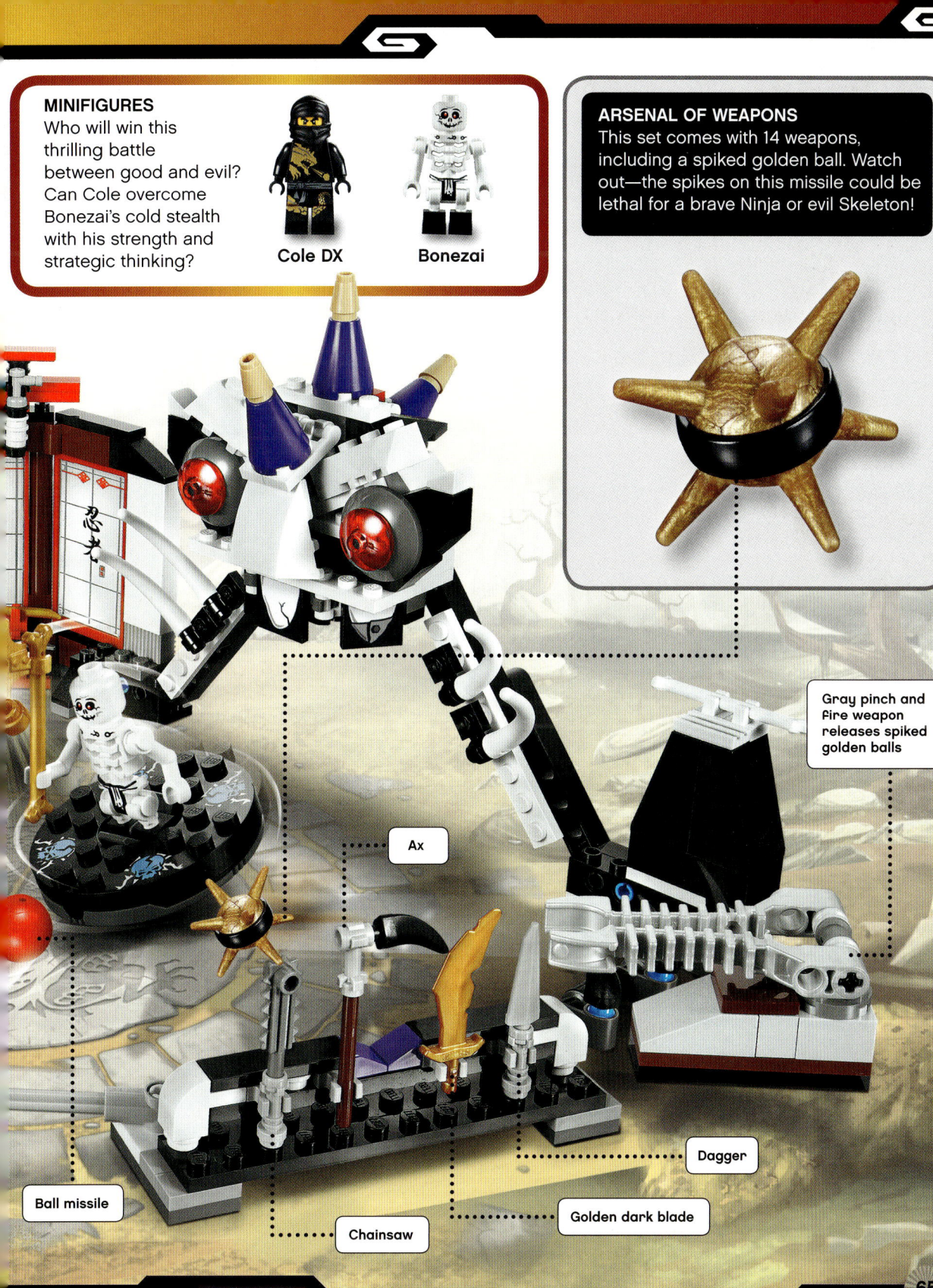

MINIFIGURES
Who will win this thrilling battle between good and evil? Can Cole overcome Bonezai's cold stealth with his strength and strategic thinking?

Cole DX

Bonezai

ARSENAL OF WEAPONS
This set comes with 14 weapons, including a spiked golden ball. Watch out—the spikes on this missile could be lethal for a brave Ninja or evil Skeleton!

Gray pinch and fire weapon releases spiked golden balls

Ax

Dagger

Ball missile

Chainsaw

Golden dark blade

65

SKELETON BOWLING

SKELETON STRIKE!

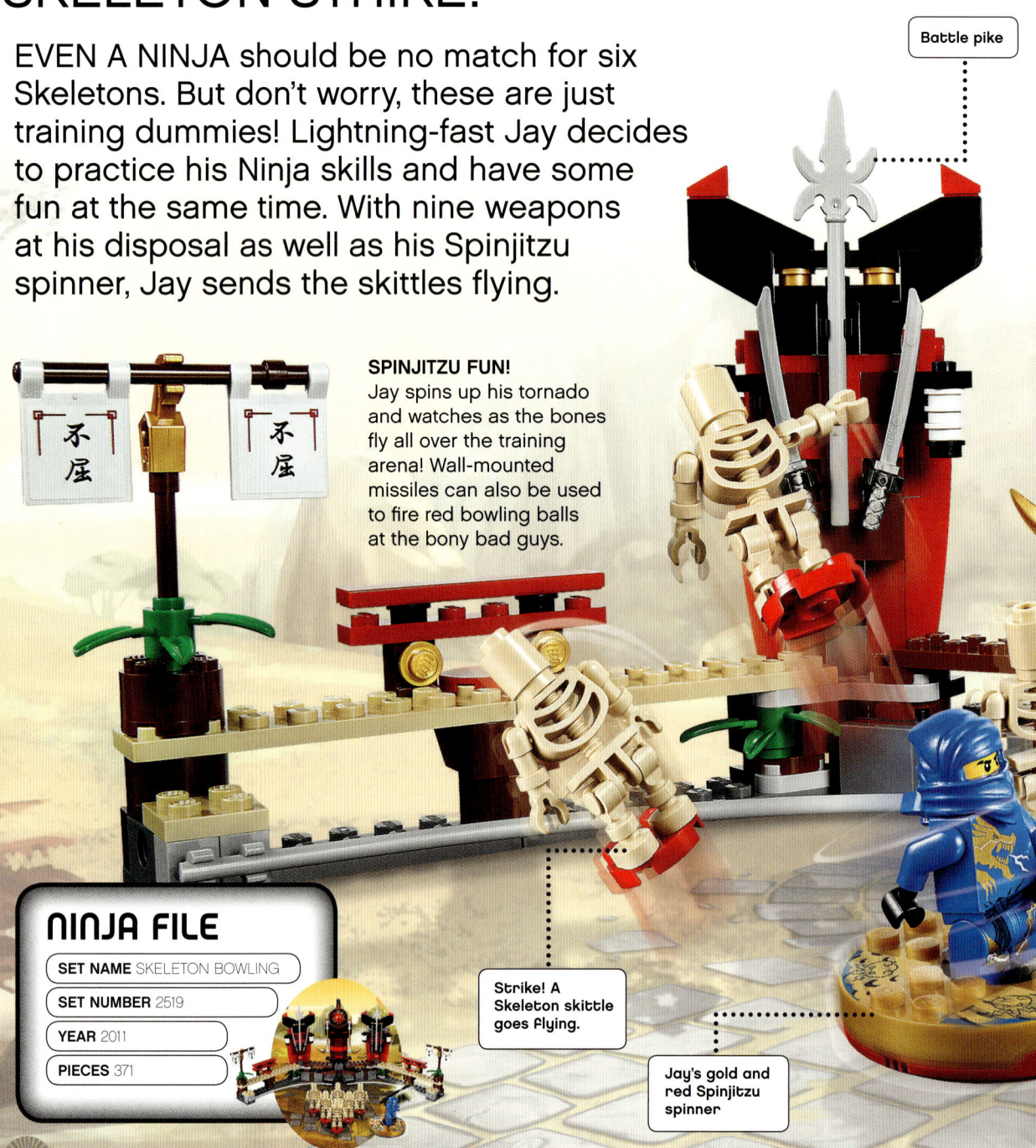

EVEN A NINJA should be no match for six Skeletons. But don't worry, these are just training dummies! Lightning-fast Jay decides to practice his Ninja skills and have some fun at the same time. With nine weapons at his disposal as well as his Spinjitzu spinner, Jay sends the skittles flying.

Battle pike

SPINJITZU FUN!
Jay spins up his tornado and watches as the bones fly all over the training arena! Wall-mounted missiles can also be used to fire red bowling balls at the bony bad guys.

Strike! A Skeleton skittle goes flying.

Jay's gold and red Spinjitzu spinner

NINJA FILE
SET NAME	SKELETON BOWLING
SET NUMBER	2519
YEAR	2011
PIECES	371

MINIFIGURES
Caught in an ambush, Jay uses his Ninja DX skills to turn the situation to his advantage. Six evil Skeletons are no match for this brave Ninja!

Jay DX

Wall-mounted flick bowling ball missile

PLAY ALONG
How good is your Skeleton bowling? Keep score on this rotating board. If you hit all six Skeletons, turn the dial to the skull symbol. Nice bowling!

Traditional flags and plants decorate the arena.

KRUNCHA
GENERAL OF EARTH

LOUD, HARD, AND strong, Kruncha is one of the four Generals in the Skeleton Army. He is constantly bickering with General Nuckal. Kruncha is mean and will crush anyone who dares to get in his way.

NINJA FILE
- **SET NAME** KRUNCHA
- **SET NUMBER** 2174
- **YEAR** 2011
- **PIECES** 24

Kruncha wears a monocle on his right eye.

Chest plate with added protection for Skeleton Generals

WEAPONS

CHAINED FANG
A dinosaur tooth on a steel chain is perfect for piercing an enemy in battle.

GOLDEN HATCHET TWINS
This double-bladed golden weapon is twice as deadly as a regular ax.

BONE
Every Skeleton likes to have a big bone weapon to wield in battle.

BODY ARMOR
Kruncha's protective body armor is different from that of most other Skeletons. The shoulder pads are heavier and he doesn't wear the gray chest panel with markings on it. Only Wyplash has similar armor to Kruncha's.

ROCK HARD SPINJITZU

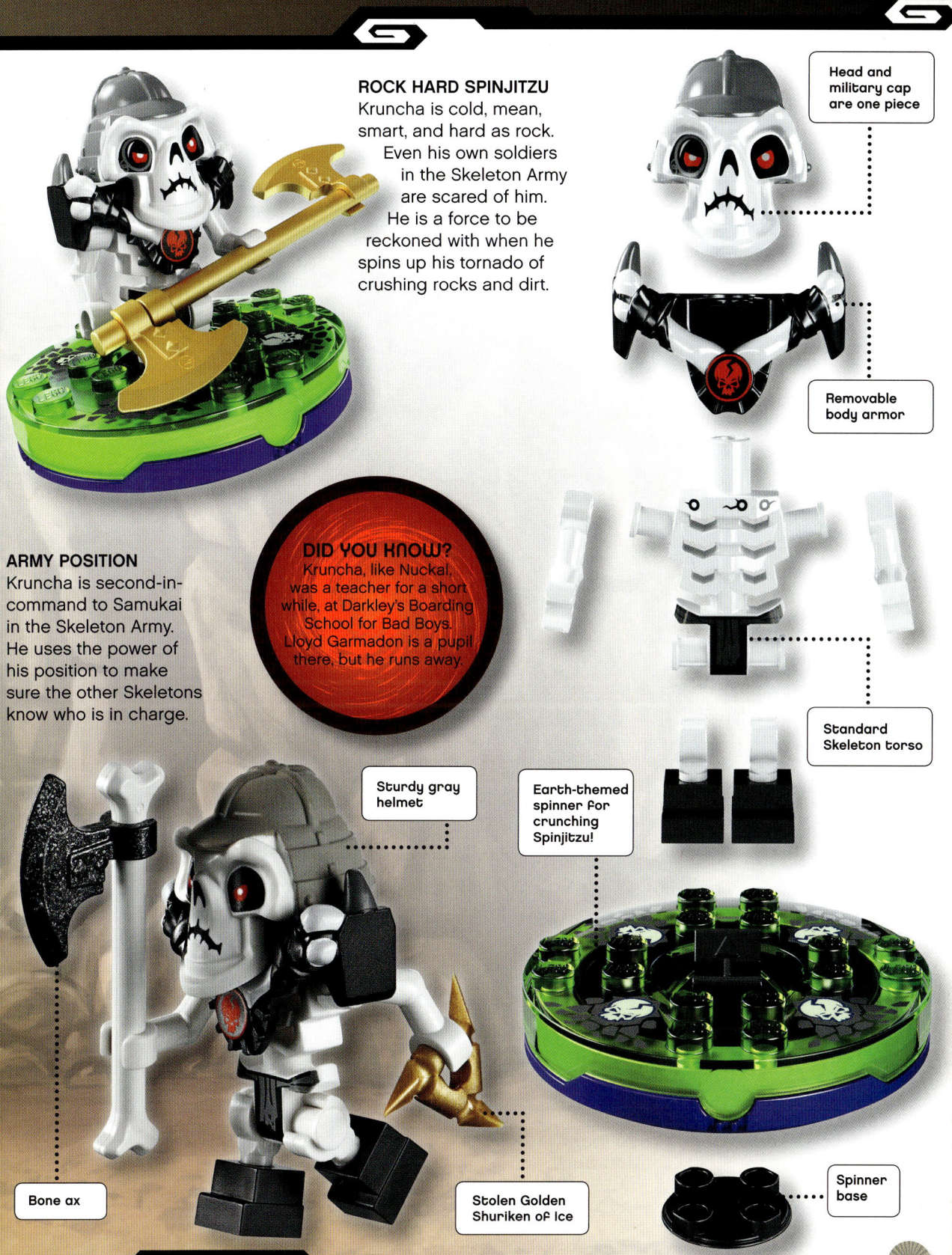

Kruncha is cold, mean, smart, and hard as rock. Even his own soldiers in the Skeleton Army are scared of him. He is a force to be reckoned with when he spins up his tornado of crushing rocks and dirt.

Head and military cap are one piece

Removable body armor

ARMY POSITION

Kruncha is second-in-command to Samukai in the Skeleton Army. He uses the power of his position to make sure the other Skeletons know who is in charge.

DID YOU KNOW?
Kruncha, like Nuckal, was a teacher for a short while, at Darkley's Boarding School for Bad Boys. Lloyd Garmadon is a pupil there, but he runs away.

Standard Skeleton torso

Sturdy gray helmet

Earth-themed spinner for crunching Spinjitzu!

Bone ax

Stolen Golden Shuriken of Ice

Spinner base

69

SKULLCOPTER
RESCUE MISSION

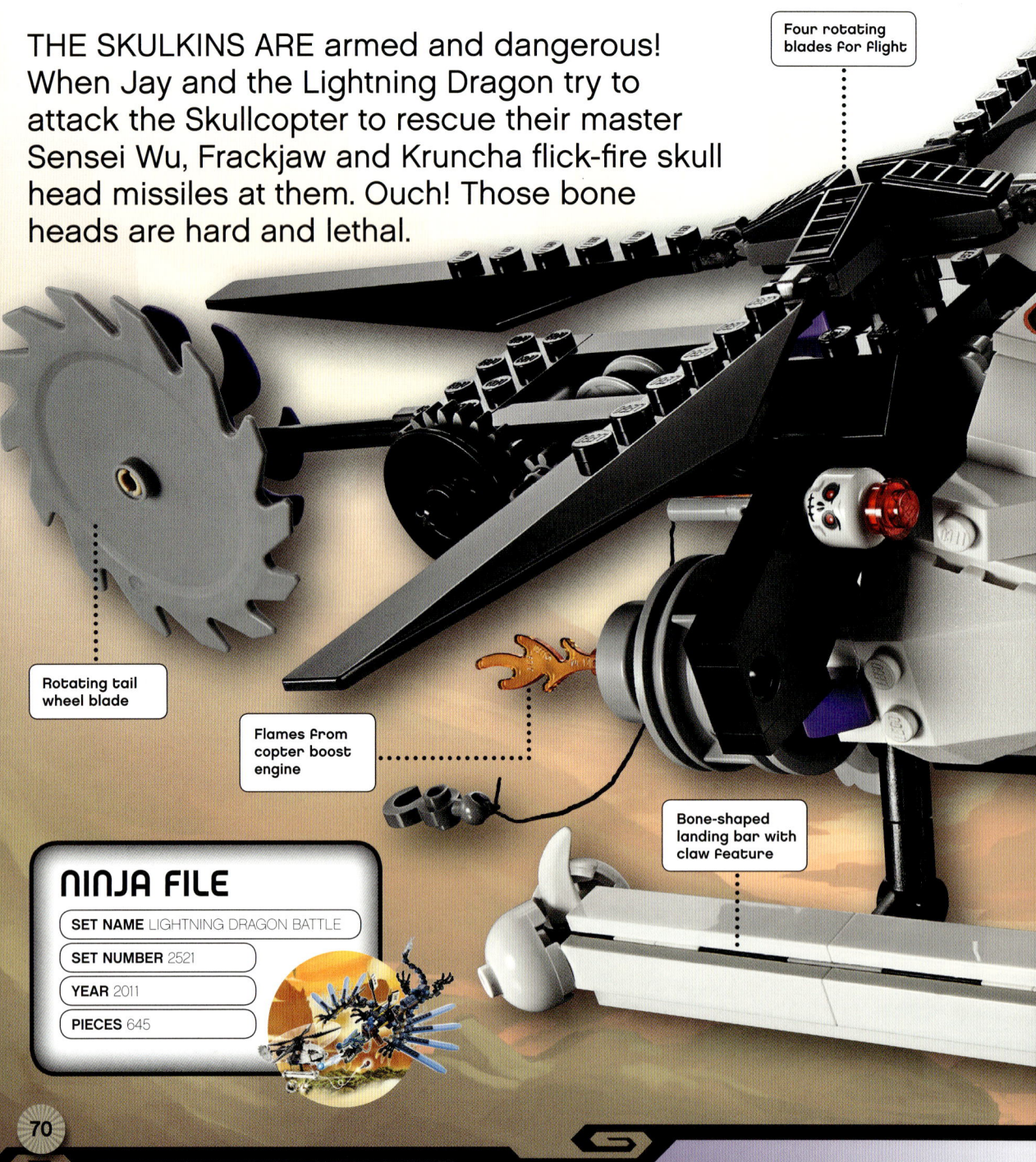

THE SKULKINS ARE armed and dangerous! When Jay and the Lightning Dragon try to attack the Skullcopter to rescue their master Sensei Wu, Frackjaw and Kruncha flick-fire skull head missiles at them. Ouch! Those bone heads are hard and lethal.

Four rotating blades for flight

Rotating tail wheel blade

Flames from copter boost engine

Bone-shaped landing bar with claw feature

NINJA FILE
SET NAME	LIGHTNING DRAGON BATTLE
SET NUMBER	2521
YEAR	2011
PIECES	645

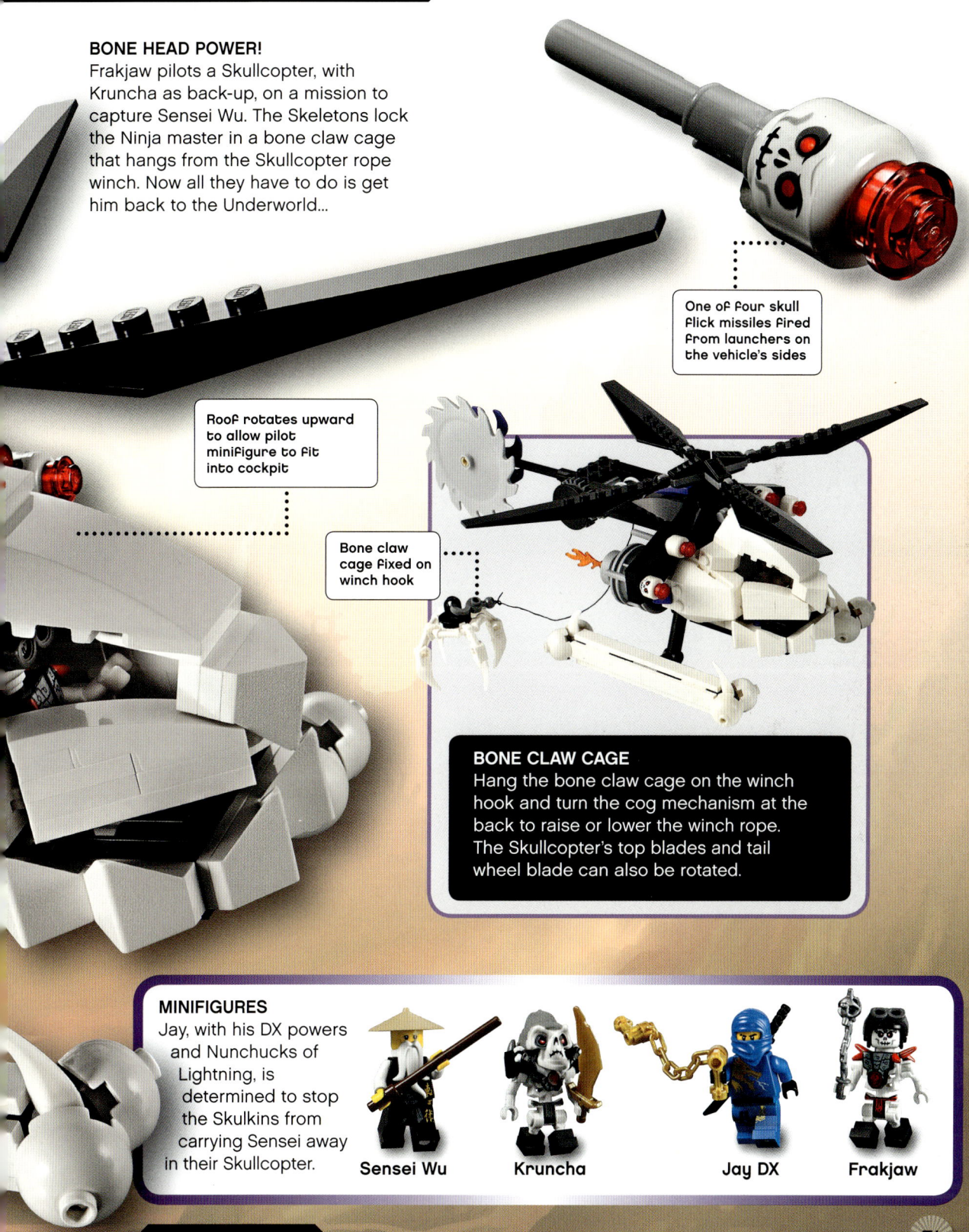

BONE HEAD POWER!
Frakjaw pilots a Skullcopter, with Kruncha as back-up, on a mission to capture Sensei Wu. The Skeletons lock the Ninja master in a bone claw cage that hangs from the Skullcopter rope winch. Now all they have to do is get him back to the Underworld...

One of four skull flick missiles fired from launchers on the vehicle's sides

Roof rotates upward to allow pilot minifigure to fit into cockpit

Bone claw cage fixed on winch hook

BONE CLAW CAGE
Hang the bone claw cage on the winch hook and turn the cog mechanism at the back to raise or lower the winch rope. The Skullcopter's top blades and tail wheel blade can also be rotated.

MINIFIGURES
Jay, with his DX powers and Nunchucks of Lightning, is determined to stop the Skulkins from carrying Sensei away in their Skullcopter.

Sensei Wu   **Kruncha**   **Jay DX**   **Frakjaw**

71

WYPLASH
GENERAL OF ICE

THIS FEARSOME SKELETON is a General in Garmadon's Army. He even takes control of the Army in Samukai's absence. Stealth is his special skill, and he always watches and waits for the right moment to attack his enemy.

DID YOU KNOW? Wyplash can turn his huge skull backward! This is a useful skill when you are as paranoid as he is—he can always see the enemy approaching.

Traditional bamboo hat

Bone spikes make armor look more terrifying

Shoulder pad and body protection armor

UNDERWORLD SPY
Wyplash is so stealthy that he can creep up on his enemies unseen. This makes him an ideal spy. He watches and listens, gathering information to plan an attack or set up an ambush.

NINJA FILE
SET NAME	WYPLASH
SET NUMBER	2175
YEAR	2011
PIECES	23

WEAPONS

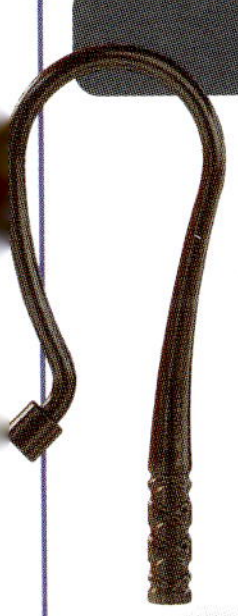

GROOVY WHIP
As his name suggests, Wyplash is an expert at using his whip to attack and capture his enemies.

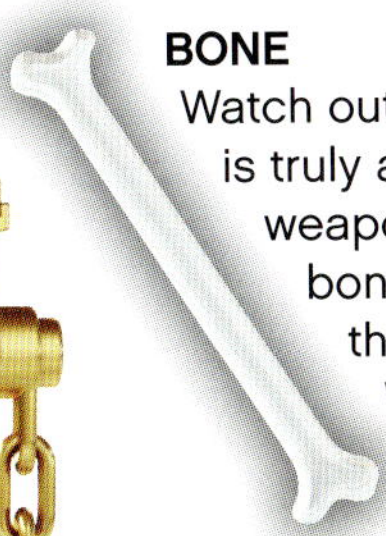

BONE
Watch out! This bone is truly a lethal weapon in the bony hands of the fearsome Wyplash.

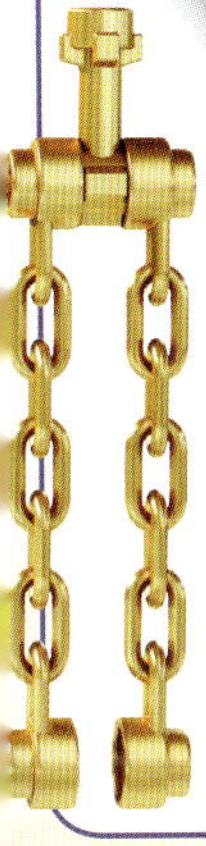

GOLDEN HELI-CHAINS
When these vicious chains are swung in the air they sound like the swoosh of metallic wings!

ICE TORNADO
Wyplash can spin up a chaotic Ice tornado. Combined with the force of his heli-chains, it makes him unstoppable. He wants nothing more than to destroy the living!

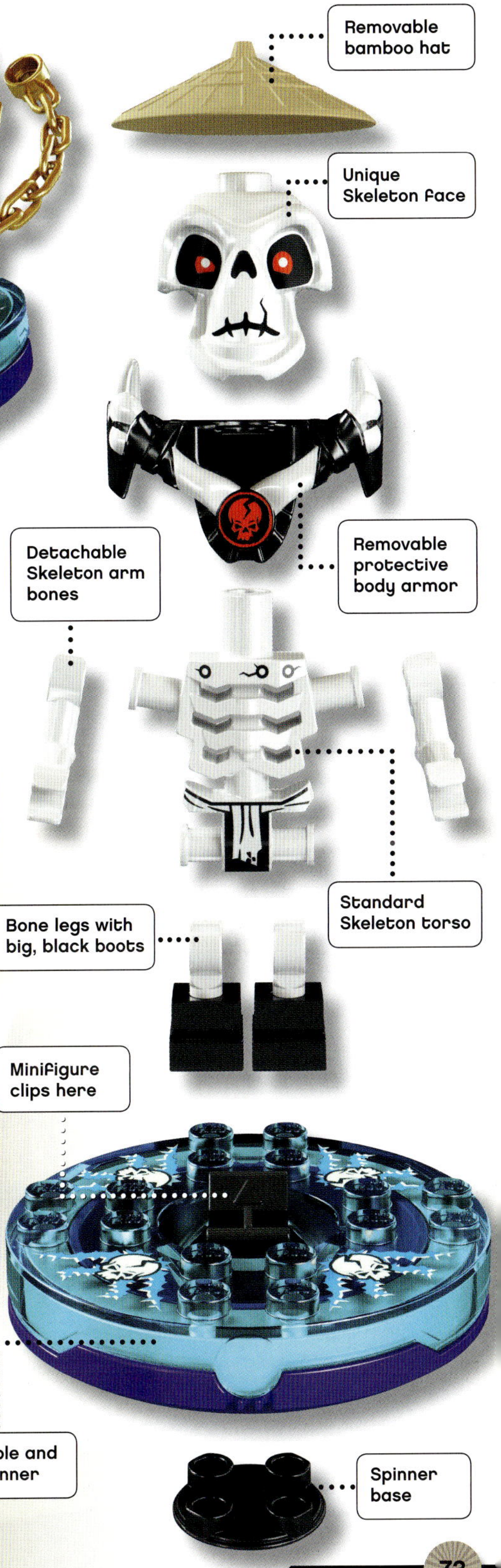

Removable bamboo hat

Unique Skeleton face

Detachable Skeleton arm bones

Removable protective body armor

Hole in skull with worm crawling out

Bone legs with big, black boots

Standard Skeleton torso

Minifigure clips here

Bone ax

Icy purple and blue spinner

Spinner base

SKULL DECORATION
Wyplash is the only Skeleton who has a worm crawling from a hole in the side of his skull!

SKULL TRUCK

MONSTER VEHICLE

THE MONSTROUS Skull Truck is intended to scare even the bravest Ninja. Its hood takes the form of a skull, with jaws that can chomp down on anything or anyone that gets in the way. And if the jaws don't catch them, then the bone fist missile might!

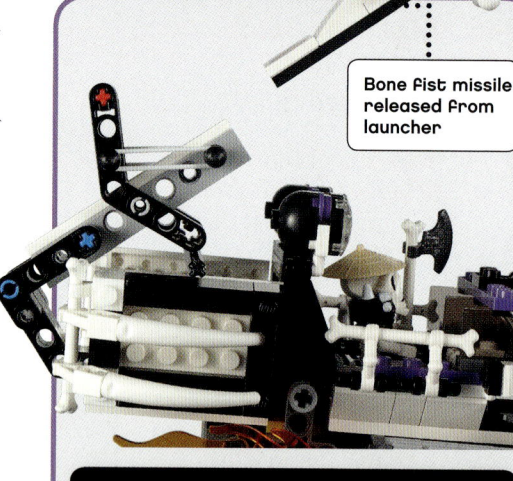

Bone fist missile released from launcher

BONE LAUNCHER
Position, aim, and pull down on the moving hinged launcher device at the back of the Skull Truck to let loose the hard-hitting bone fist missile!

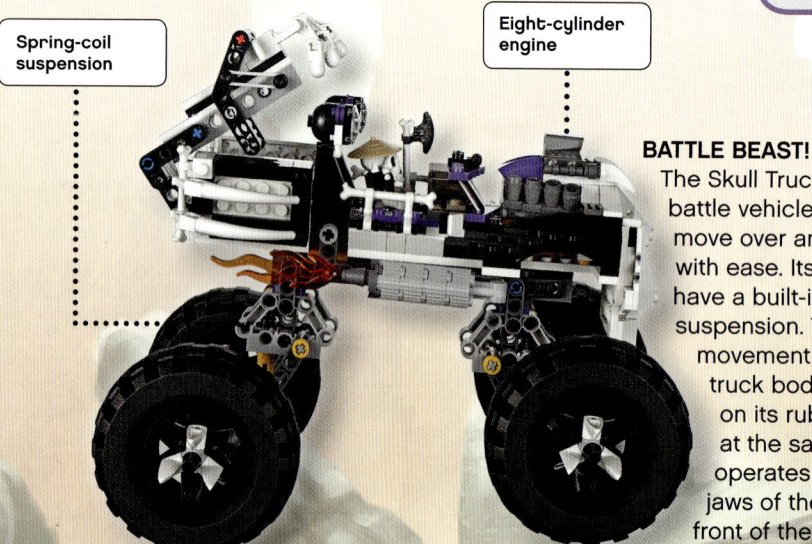

Spring-coil suspension

Eight-cylinder engine

Large, all-terrain rubber tires

BATTLE BEAST!
The Skull Truck is an ideal battle vehicle as it can move over any terrain with ease. Its huge wheels have a built-in spring-coil suspension. The springing movement pushes the truck body up and down on its rubber tires and, at the same time, operates the crushing jaws of the skull at the front of the vehicle.

MINIFIGURES
Lord Garmadon and Wyplash are escaping in the Skull Truck with the Nunchucks of Lightning. Can Jay and Zane stop them?

Wyplash  — **Jay**  — **Zane** 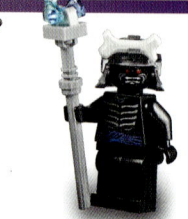  — **Lord Garmadon**

NINJA FILE

SET NAME	SKULL TRUCK
SET NUMBER	2506
YEAR	2011
PIECES	515

Bone fist missile fires from launcher

Movable hinged bone launcher

Wyplash slots into the cockpit to drive his Skull Truck.

Giant teeth prison cage (one on either side of truck)

Skull jaws chomp up and down

PRISONER TRANSPORTATION
The bone teeth cages at the back of the Truck are ideal for transporting enemy prisoners. Lift the bone bars and place a minifigure into the base, and then push the teeth back down to lock in the captive.

NUCKAL

GENERAL OF LIGHTNING

NUCKAL IS CHILDISH, wild, and very dangerous. He loves fighting, and if there is trouble to be found, Nuckal will find it! Watch out Ninja—this bony brute can strike you down with his lightning-fast moves and his bony battle skills.

DID YOU KNOW?
The four Skeleton Generals, Nuckal, Samukai, Wyplash, and Kruncha are the only Skeleton minifigures to have proper skull-shaped head pieces.

Unique row of head spikes

Blue shoulder spikes, part of protective body armor

Huge, distinctive skull-shaped head

Skeleton Army emblem

Bone legs with black boots clipped to torso

NINJA FILE

SET NAME	NUCKAL
SET NUMBER	2173
YEAR	2011
PIECES	26

SMASHING FUN!
Nuckal loves having fun, but his idea of fun is fighting and smashing things up! His cackling and electrifying laugh is terrifying, especially when he is wielding a lethal weapon at the same time.

WEAPONS

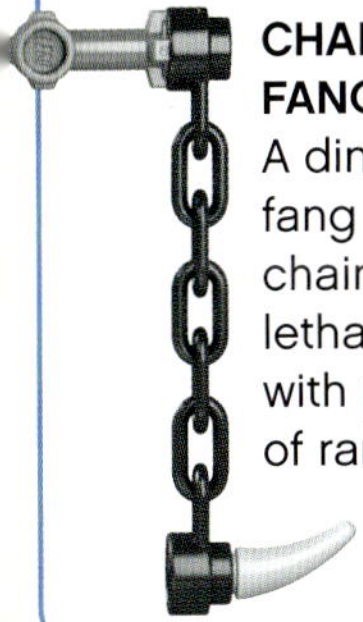

CHAINED FANG
A dinosaur fang on a chain makes a lethal weapon with plenty of range.

SILVER DARK BLADE
This short, curved blade was created especially for the Skeleton Army.

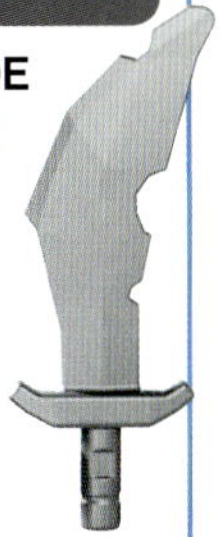

GOLDEN DOUBLE-BLADED BONE AX
Twin blades give this gleaming ax twice the slicing power.

Nuckal has only one eye—he lost the other in battle.

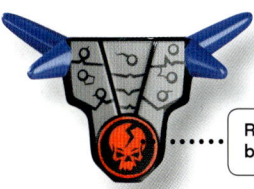

Removable body armor

SPINJITZU GENERAL
Nuckal is the only Skeleton General minifigure whose spinner is not transparent. He spins up electrifying Lightning tornadoes with his silver and blue spinner.

Skeleton torso, with pattern of holes and cracks

Standard army issue sash printed on torso

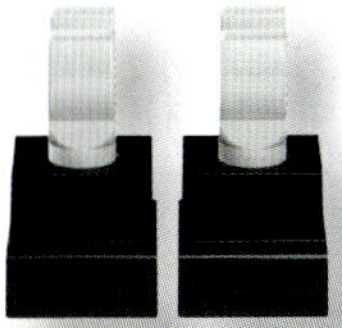

FURIOUS FIGHTER
Armed with a heavy bone ax and a jagged silver dark blade, this variant Nuckal minifigure does what he does best—fight. His moves are lightning-fast and furious. Be afraid, very afraid!

Bone ax

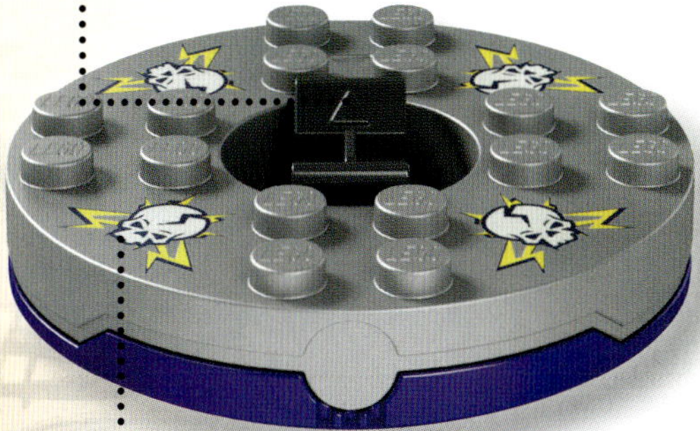

Minifigure clips here.

Lightning Skeleton Army symbol

Spinner base

77

NUCKAL'S ATV

MISSION IMPOSSIBLE?

NINJA, WATCH OUT! Nuckal's monster All-Terrain Vehicle (ATV) causes maximum destruction wherever it goes. This scary bone buggy packs a punch with its heavy armor, solid suspension, and missile launcher. It is to be avoided at all costs!

NINJA FILE
- **SET NAME** NUCKAL'S ATV
- **SET NUMBER** 2518
- **YEAR** 2011
- **PIECES** 174

MINIFIGURES
Nuckal is trying to capture Nya. Can Kai use his Spinjitzu skills to stop Nuckal and save his sister?

Nuckal

Kai DX

ALL-TERRAIN VEHICLE
Nuckal certainly has the advantage on the battlefield with this terrifying four-wheeled vehicle. The ATV has full body armor for protection, and a missile launcher for causing serious damage. The spiked wheels and suspension mean Nuckal can tear up and over any terrain.

Empty missile launcher

Skull hood piece moves up and down

Fiery exhaust flame

Missile loaded in launcher

Twin fang bone ax

BUILT TO BATTLE
Nuckal's favorite pastime is fighting and smashing things up, so this is the perfect vehicle for him. With his lightning-fast agility, he can maneuver this bony beast of a machine with skill and precision!

Decorative bone tusks move on hinges

Rocket torpedo missile

ALL-TERRAIN MISSILES
Aim and hit the red button behind the skull head to launch this lethal rocket torpedo. Kai will have to use all his Ninja skills to avoid this explosive device.

Large spiked armored all-terrain wheels

79

DARK FORTRESS

GARMADON'S LAIR

THE SCENE IS set for an epic battle between good and evil. The Ninja must rescue three of the Golden Weapons, but will they get past the terrifying defenses of Lord Garmadon's Underworld Fortress?

MOVING THRONE
Only the Lord of Evil could have a flying bone throne! Garmadon will be hot on the Ninja's trail with this flame powered vehicle, if they manage to escape...

GRAVE SURPRISE!
The Fortress is full of horrible surprises! Be prepared for a bony scare if you press on the red hinge—up pops a skeleton. Argh!

Flick hinge to push skeleton out of his tomb.

Movable bone spider leg

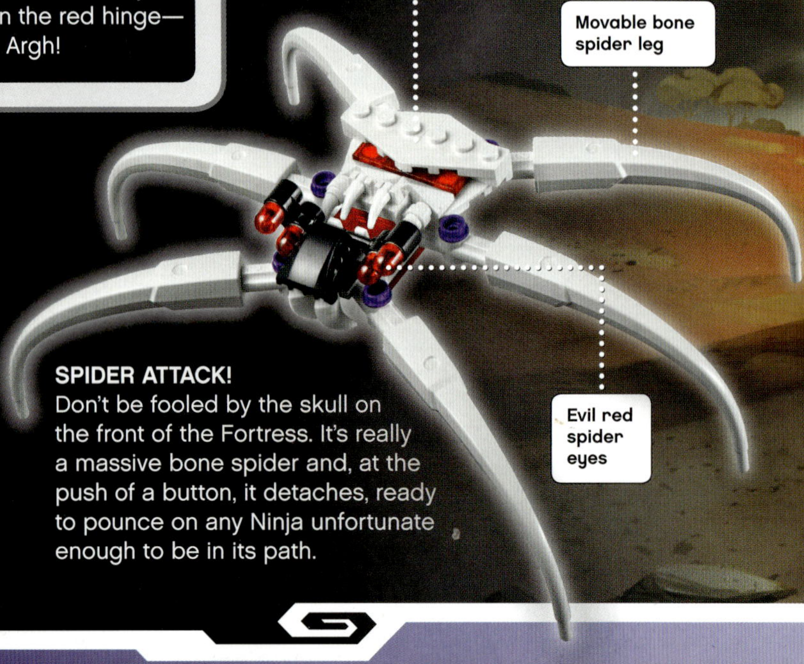

SPIDER ATTACK!
Don't be fooled by the skull on the front of the Fortress. It's really a massive bone spider and, at the push of a button, it detaches, ready to pounce on any Ninja unfortunate enough to be in its path.

Evil red spider eyes

NINJA FILE

SET NAME	Garmadon's Dark Fortress
SET NUMBER	2505
YEAR	2011
PIECES	518

MINIFIGURES
Kai and Nya will have to use all their skills to get past the Fortress's massive spider and flick missiles before they battle the Skeletons.

Chopov | Nya | Samukai | Kai | Bonezai | Lord Garmadon

Spin the tower to make Bonezai flick-fire the skull thrower missiles!

Garmadon's enemies get locked away in the tower dungeons.

Rib cage bone drawbridge

EVIL LAIR
Buried deep in the Underworld, Lord Garmadon's Fortress is filled with evil secrets and sinister shadows.

WEAPONS

BOTH THE NINJA warriors and the Skeleton Army have an incredible collection of weapons. It takes special skills to wield them and lots of practice to master them. Before going into battle a Ninja or Skeleton must evaluate his enemy and decide which weapon, or weapons, will help him win.

MACES

Golden battle mace

Silver battle mace

Swing these spikes at your foe, but be careful not to hit yourself!

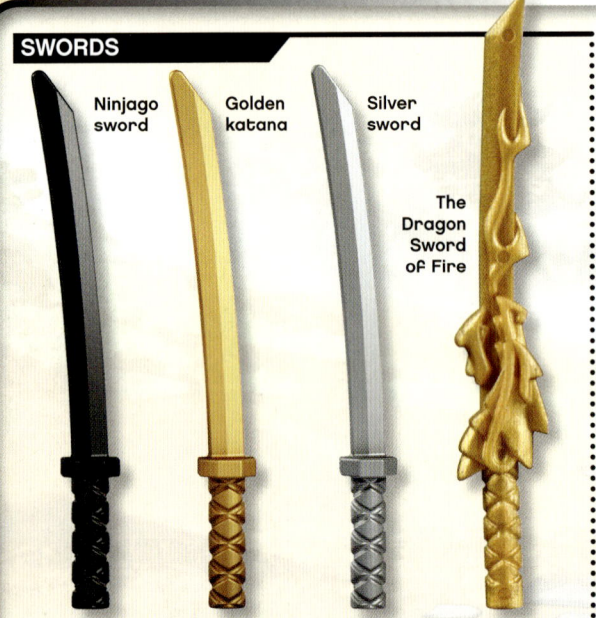

SWORDS

Ninjago sword

Golden katana

Silver sword

The Dragon Sword of Fire

The katana sword is a traditional Ninja weapon and must only be used by experts.

DARK BLADES

Dark blade

Golden dark blade

Silver dark blade

These jagged blades are more stylish than a regular dagger but also much heavier!

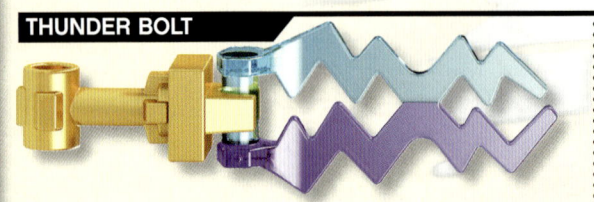

THUNDER BOLT

Made from two bolts of lightning, this sizzling weapon can sometimes be too hot to handle.

SCYTHE BLADE

This curved blade is more commonly seen on a longer scythe weapon.

AXES

Golden double-bladed bone ax

Silver bone ax

Golden bone ax

Golden hatchet twins

Trusty ax

Chop chop! These trusty old weapons can also be used to chop firewood.

DARK TALONS

These weapons fit over a minifigure's hands for close combat situations.

SPEARS

Basic spear

Golden spear

Silver spear

Icicle spear

Battle pike

PICKAXES

Grim pickax

Golden pickax

Axes make an excellent weapon or a useful tool.

Long and very heavy, these spears can only be wielded by the strongest Ninja or Skulkins.

SCYTHES

Scythe of Quakes

Double-boned skeli-scythe

Double-bladed scythe

Bone scythe

Scythes can be used for cutting down crops on the field, or opponents on the battlefield.

DAGGERS

Golden nick dagger

Silver nick dagger

Dragon's breath dagger

Bone dagger

Double-bladed bone dagger

Double-bladed dagger

BLACKSMITH'S HAMMER

Blunt and heavy, a hammer is great for banging in nails, or whacking enemies on the head.

SHURIKENS OF ICE

Beware of these beautiful throwing stars, they are extremely sharp!

Gold-tipped, breathing fire, or double-bladed, there is a dagger to suit every kind of battle!

BONES

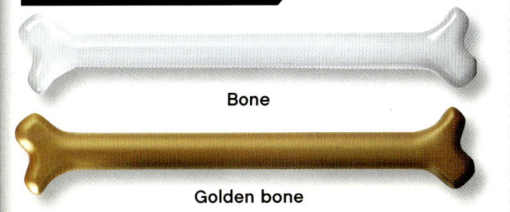

Bone

Golden bone

A Skeleton favorite, bones are brilliant for bashing and banging.

STAFFS

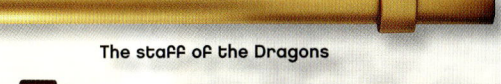

The staff of the Dragons

Nin-jô staff

Staffs are simple weapons and if you are not in a battle, they make a handy walking stick.

CHAIN SAW

Stay away from this sharp, buzzing weapon, unless you have a tree to cut down.

GROOVY WHIP

This is made from a vicious vine that grasps its victims and never lets go!

CHAIN WEAPONS

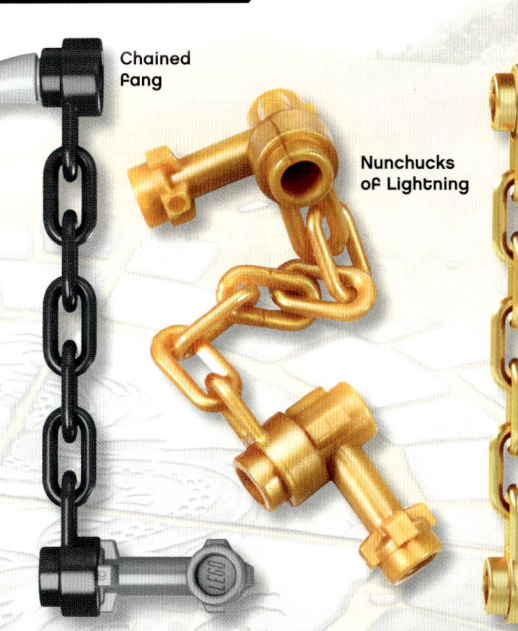

Chained Fang

Nunchucks of Lightning

Golden heli-chains

Dark chained whip

Golden chained Fang

Swirl and whirl these chains to wrap them around your target. But try not to get tangled up in them yourself!

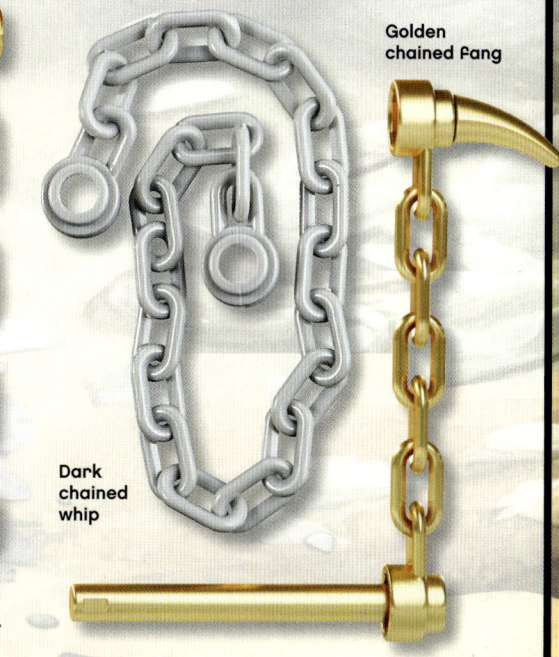

FINAL BATTLE AT THE DARK FORTRESS

THE SKELETONS HAVE stolen three of the Golden Weapons. Sensei Wu and the Ninja bravely go to Lord Garmadon's Underworld lair to get them back. They must stop the dark Lord uniting all four Weapons and destroying Ninjago.

ATTACK! The Ninja confront the Skeleton Army at Lord Garmadon's Dark Fortress. The Skeletons have an arsenal of evil weapons and missiles. Watch out for the skull thrower missiles, Ninja!

FIGHT! During an epic battle between the Skeletons and the Ninja, the clever Ninja combine their elemental powers to make a mighty Tornado of Creation. With Nya's help, they destroy the Skeleton Army and make their way to Garmadon's Fortress throne room. Bye bye you bags of bones!

DUEL! Sensei Wu and Samukai fight for possession of the four Golden Weapons. Samukai wins. However, the combined power of the Weapons is too great, and Samukai is destroyed. So long, Samukai!

Garmadon escapes into the vortex on his flying throne.

The Dark Fortress

Kai spins a fiery tornado.

Samukai battles for possession of the four Golden Weapons.

UH OH! The awesome power of the Golden Weapons opens up a mysterious vortex to another world. Lord Garmadon escapes into this vortex. But don't worry, he'll be back to get revenge on his brother one day…

NINJA VS. SERPENTINE

SEASON TWO OF LEGO® Ninjago sees the return of Lord Garmadon from the Underworld. Plus, a new enemy is unleashed—the Serpentine. A total of fourteen amazing LEGO sets bring the action to life. Turn the page and learn about all the characters, weapons, vehicles, and locations—and meet a very special Ninja...

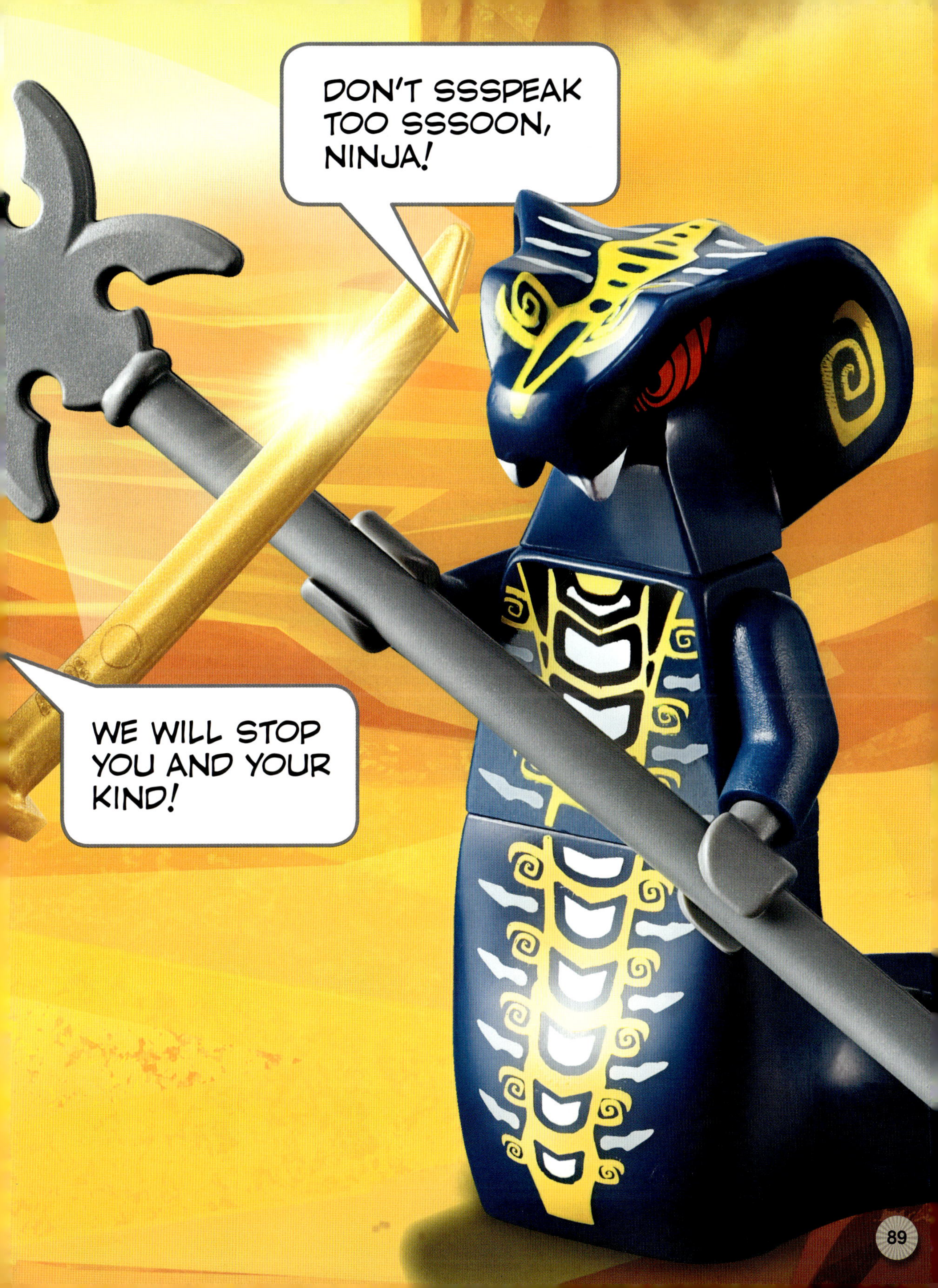
DON'T SSSPEAK TOO SSSOON, NINJA!
WE WILL STOP YOU AND YOUR KIND!

A NEW ADVENTURE

Peace in the land of Ninjago did not last very long. Lord Garmadon has returned from the Underworld. This time he is stronger than before and has the power to control all four Golden Weapons. But the Ninja are stronger too, and Cole, Jay, Kai, and Zane will do everything they can to protect these powerful Weapons...

LLOYD GARMADON

While Lord Garmadon lurks in the shadows, waiting for the right moment to strike, the Ninja meet his young son, Lloyd Garmadon. The mischievous Lloyd carelessly unleashes a fearsome new enemy upon Ninjago—the mysterious and ancient Serpentine tribes.

THE GREAT DEVOURER

FANG BLADES

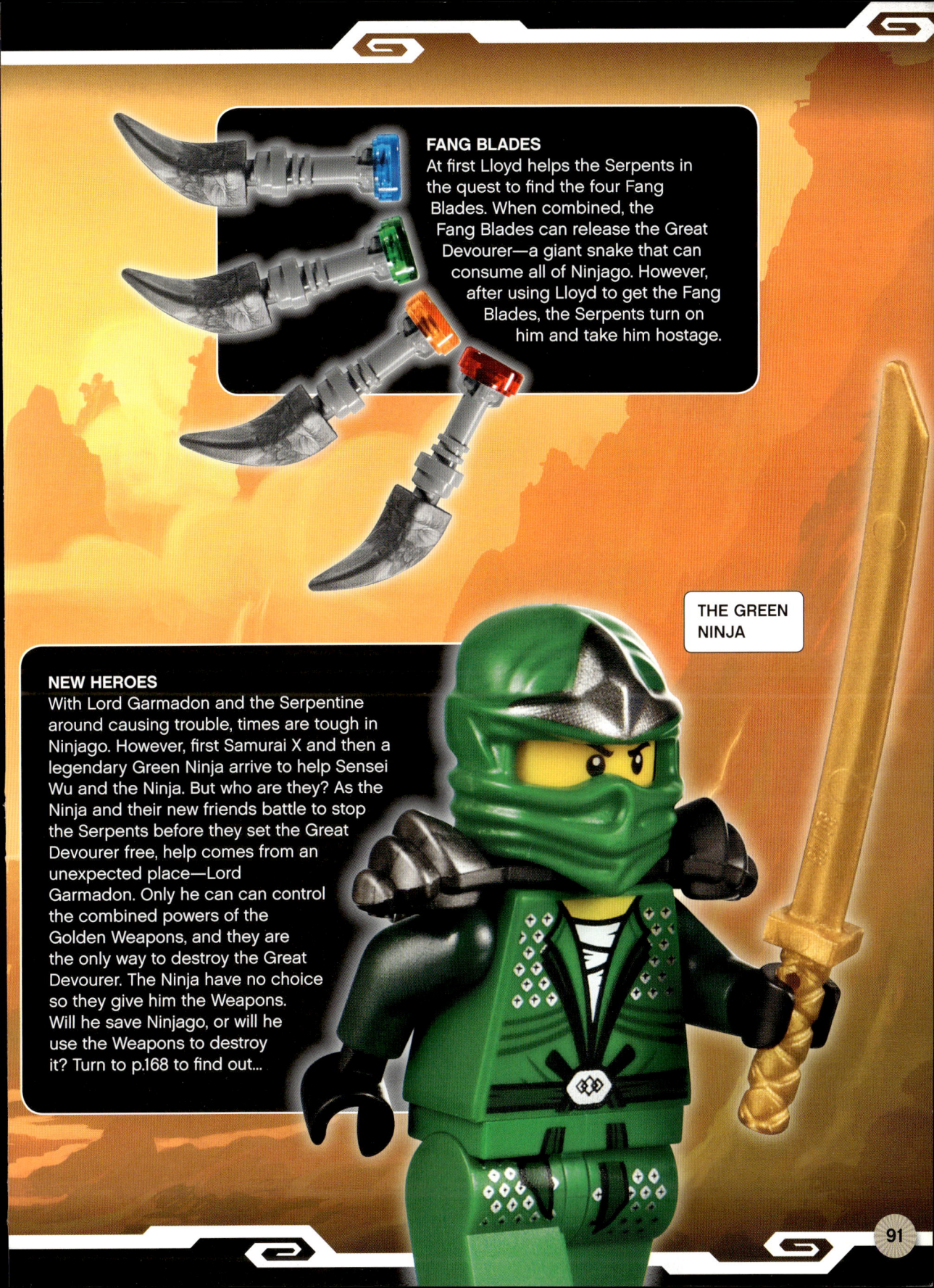

At first Lloyd helps the Serpents in the quest to find the four Fang Blades. When combined, the Fang Blades can release the Great Devourer—a giant snake that can consume all of Ninjago. However, after using Lloyd to get the Fang Blades, the Serpents turn on him and take him hostage.

THE GREEN NINJA

NEW HEROES

With Lord Garmadon and the Serpentine around causing trouble, times are tough in Ninjago. However, first Samurai X and then a legendary Green Ninja arrive to help Sensei Wu and the Ninja. But who are they? As the Ninja and their new friends battle to stop the Serpents before they set the Great Devourer free, help comes from an unexpected place—Lord Garmadon. Only he can can control the combined powers of the Golden Weapons, and they are the only way to destroy the Great Devourer. The Ninja have no choice so they give him the Weapons. Will he save Ninjago, or will he use the Weapons to destroy it? Turn to p.168 to find out…

SENSEI WU

NINJA TEACHER

THE CALM AND self-disciplined Sensei Wu is the perfect teacher. After years of training, he knows what it takes to master Spinjitzu and the Elements. He uses this knowledge to teach the Ninja and help them to reach the next three levels—ZX (Zen eXtreme), Kendo, and NRG.

Traditional conical bamboo sun hat

"Sensei" mustache and beard

Sensei Wu's alternative white robes feature snake symbols to protect him from evil.

Gray obi sash belt

NINJA FILE
SET NAME	DESTINY'S BOUNTY
SET NUMBER	9446
YEAR	2012
PIECES	684

MASTER OF THE ELEMENTS
Sensei Wu knows how to bring out the best in the young Ninja. He trains each of them in one of the four Elements of Ninjago—Earth, Lightning, Fire, or Ice. The four Elements are powerful forces that can be harnessed for good or evil. The Ninja can control these Elements, but so can the evil Lord Garmadon and his Skeleton Army.

THE FOUR ELEMENTS
Each Ninja is assigned one of the Elements and must train hard to master it. Sensei Wu identifies the Ninja's individual skills and helps them harness the Elements in their own way.

FIRE
Kai's elemental power is Fire. His personality is wild and intense like a fire. He can be reckless and impatient and quick to anger.

EARTH
Cole's elemental power is Earth. He may be a bit gruff, but he is strong, focused, reliable, and solid as a rock.

DID YOU KNOW?
Lord Garmadon has the ability to command all four of the Elements, just like his little brother, Sensei Wu. Unlike Wu, however, Garmadon's grasp of the elemental forces is unbalanced, a sign of his inner evil.

LIGHTNING
Jay's elemental power is Lightning. He is creative, brave, has a great sense of humor, and is lightning-fast in combat.

ICE
Zane's elemental power is Ice. He is serious, stealthy, and focused. He is always cool under pressure.

DESTINY'S BOUNTY

NINJA HEADQUARTERS

DESTINY'S BOUNTY IS the Ninja's new home and training center. The dragon-themed ship comes fully equipped with a cannon with a 360 degree firing range, four crossbows, two concealed weapon compartments, and a hidden treasure chest with jewels inside. All aboard!

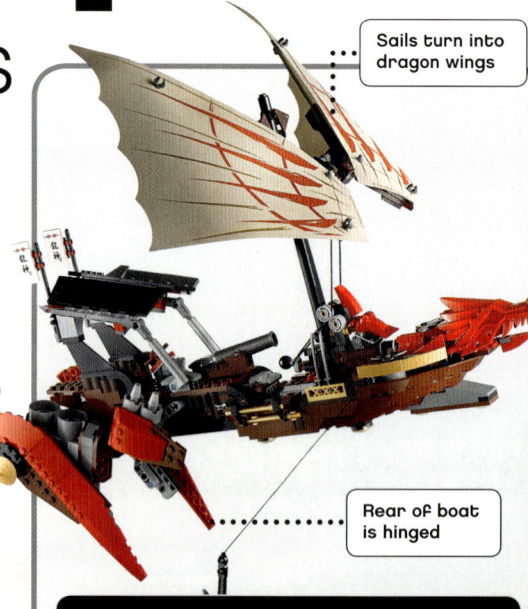

Sails turn into dragon wings

Rear of boat is hinged

NINJA FILE
SET NAME	DESTINY'S BOUNTY
SET NUMBER	9446
YEAR	2012
PIECES	684

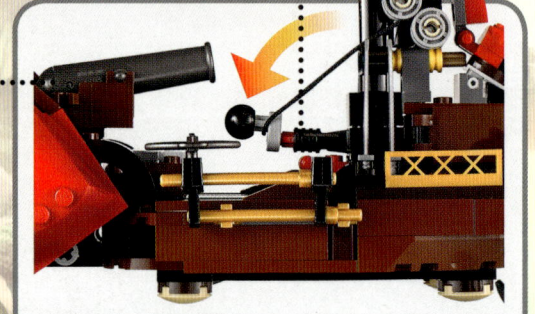

DESTINY JET
Destiny's Bounty hides a few surprises—the stern (rear end) twists down to convert the ship into a flying machine. The red blade-like side panels become the booster engines to power the Destiny Jet.

Lever to open and close sails

Pull lever on back of cannon to launch missiles.

Fired cannonball!

LEVERAGE
A clever system of ropes and pulleys, operated by a turning lever, opens and closes the sails for flight or sail mode.

Dragon figurehead mouth snaps open and closed

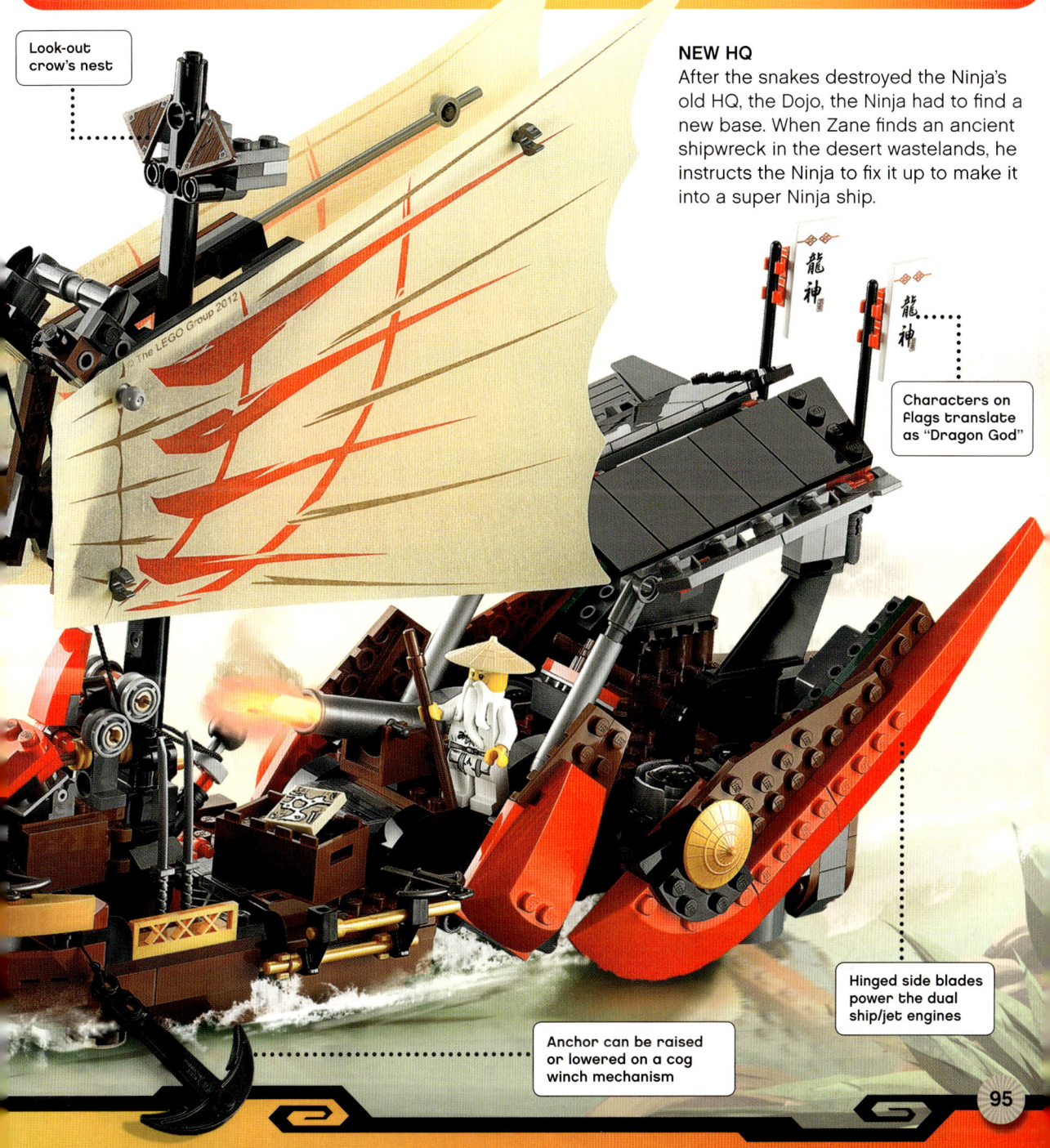

MINIFIGURES
The armed Ninja use their new HQ to train and to plan their counter-attacks against Lord Garmadon and the Serpents.

Kendo Jay
Kendo Zane
Sensei Wu
Lord Garmadon
Skales
Slithraa

Look-out crow's nest

NEW HQ
After the snakes destroyed the Ninja's old HQ, the Dojo, the Ninja had to find a new base. When Zane finds an ancient shipwreck in the desert wastelands, he instructs the Ninja to fix it up to make it into a super Ninja ship.

Characters on flags translate as "Dragon God"

Hinged side blades power the dual ship/jet engines

Anchor can be raised or lowered on a cog winch mechanism

KAI ZX
FIRE ZEN EXTREME

SINCE BATTLING THE Skeleton Army, Kai has worked hard to achieve the next level of his Ninja training—ZX, or Zen eXtreme level. His ZX minifigure is ready to take on new challenges and enemies.

NINJA FILE
- **SET NAME** Kai ZX
- **SET NUMBER** 9561
- **YEAR** 2012
- **PIECES** 21

ZX hood features golden helmet crown

Gold shoulder pauldrons

Protective chest plate over simple red tunic

Throwing stars tucked into belt

WEAPONS

DRAGON SWORD OF FIRE
This unique weapon gives its wielder the power of Fire!

Ancient, ornate blade

SILVER SERPENT STRIKER
This pronged weapon is useful when battling the deadly snakes.

BO STAFF
This fighting staff can be used for blocks, strikes, and sweeps at an enemy.

Simple wooden staff

ZX MINIFIGURE
Kai's ZX robes are printed with protective armor, weapons, and two red belts that secure everything in place during battle.

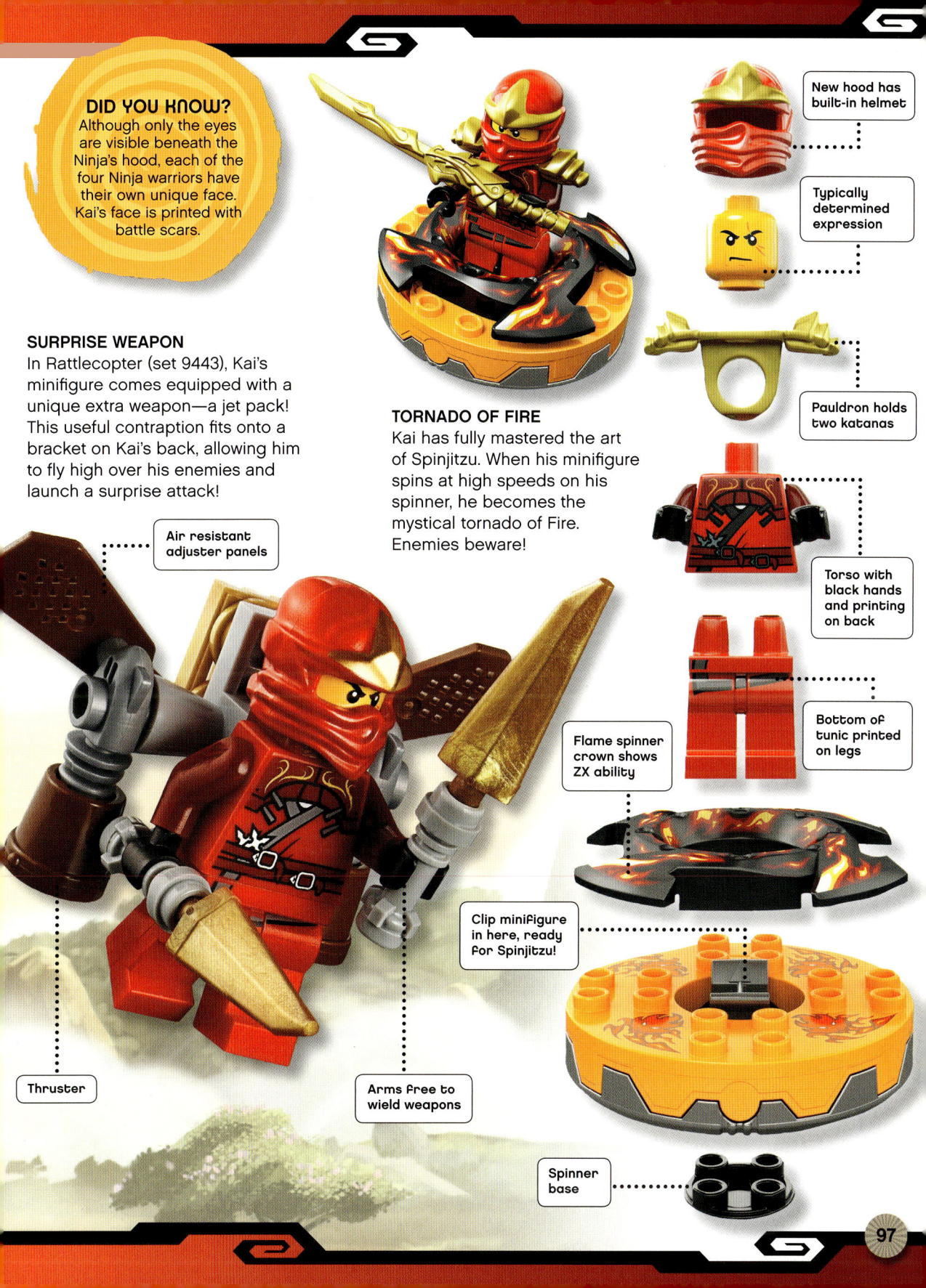

DID YOU KNOW?
Although only the eyes are visible beneath the Ninja's hood, each of the four Ninja warriors have their own unique face. Kai's face is printed with battle scars.

SURPRISE WEAPON
In Rattlecopter (set 9443), Kai's minifigure comes equipped with a unique extra weapon—a jet pack! This useful contraption fits onto a bracket on Kai's back, allowing him to fly high over his enemies and launch a surprise attack!

TORNADO OF FIRE
Kai has fully mastered the art of Spinjitzu. When his minifigure spins at high speeds on his spinner, he becomes the mystical tornado of Fire. Enemies beware!

- New hood has built-in helmet
- Typically determined expression
- Pauldron holds two katanas
- Torso with black hands and printing on back
- Bottom of tunic printed on legs
- Flame spinner crown shows ZX ability
- Clip minifigure in here, ready for Spinjitzu!
- Air resistant adjuster panels
- Thruster
- Arms free to wield weapons
- Spinner base

97

BLADE CYCLE

BATTLE OF THE BLADES

THIS FIERY VEHICLE is Kai's sleek and speedy Serpent-battling machine. The two-wheeler is perfect for chasing after sneaky snakes, such as Rattla. At the touch of a button, the sides flip out to reveal deadly blades, which are perfect for knocking over enemies.

NINJA FILE
- **SET NAME** KAI'S BLADE CYCLE
- **SET NUMBER** 9441
- **YEAR** 2012
- **PIECES** 188

Large, powerful front wheel

Kai's Fire Element symbol

Blade arm flicks out

View from above the Blade Cycle

DEADLY BLADES
Press down on the red brick in front of the handlebars to flick out two large red side pieces, with golden blades underneath. Use the yellow pointed bricks to clip the blades into place. Watch out, Rattla!

MINIFIGURES
Can Kai defeat the mind-controlling Serpent, Rattla, with his Blade Cycle's big blade attack? He must retrieve the Hypnobrai Staff and its precious anti-venom.

Kai ZX

Rattla

Kai steers this powerful machine and is ready for action!

Golden dagger blades on each side of the vehicle can spear enemies.

Press here to flip out side blades.

Tally of Serpents defeated!

IN ACTION!
Rattla has stolen the Hypnobrai Staff and its anti-venom, so Kai gives chase on his Blade Cycle. Will he be able to catch the slippery Serpent and knock him down with the side-projecting battle blades?

Golden blade can be flipped out or unclipped for hand-to-hand combat.

Yellow brick secures blades in place

Wheelie! Kai can drive the Blade Cycle just on the back wheel.

JAY ZX
LIGHTNING ZEN EXTREME

JAY HAS LEARNED many new skills from his teacher and master, Sensei Wu. His dedication to learning the ancient martial arts has certainly earned Jay his ZX Ninja status. This agile warrior is always ready to use his skills in the battle to save the world of Ninjago.

DID YOU KNOW?
Jay has a secret crush on Nya. When he cuts himself on a Fangpyre fossil skeleton and starts to turn into a snake, a kiss from Nya cures him and allows him to reach his full Ninja potential.

New hood with silver detail

Ninja headwrap conceals Jay's identity

Protective silver shoulder pauldrons

New robes feature one arm covered with protective silver armor

ZX ROBES
Jay's new robes don't just look good, they help him to be even more agile on the battlefield. The light armor is flexible, so he can look from side to side easily. He can also hide small weapons, such as daggers, in the folds of his clothes, and carry two katana blades on his back

NINJA FILE
- SET NAME JAY ZX
- SET NUMBER 9553
- YEAR 2012
- PIECES 28

100

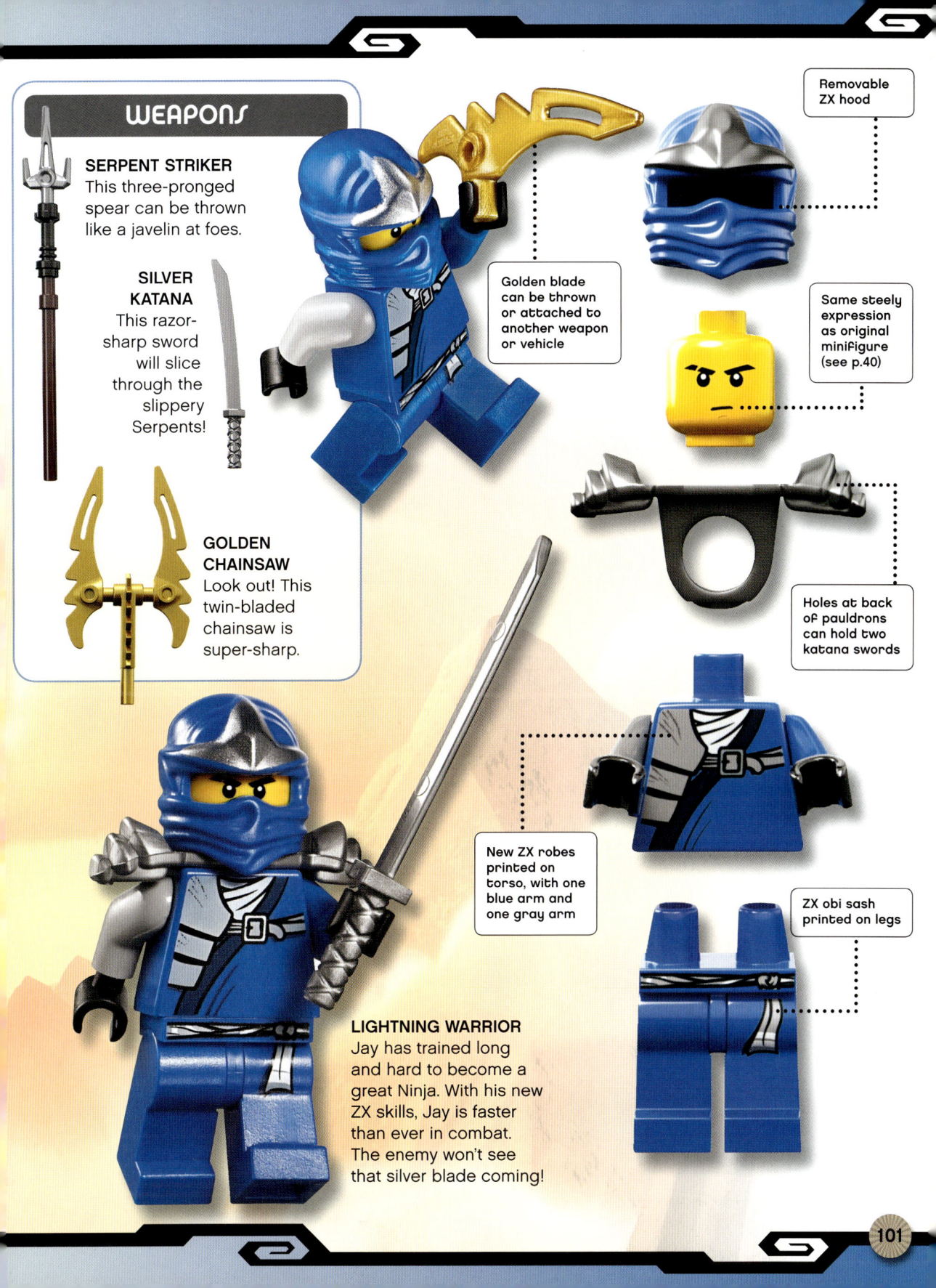

WEAPONS

SERPENT STRIKER
This three-pronged spear can be thrown like a javelin at foes.

SILVER KATANA
This razor-sharp sword will slice through the slippery Serpents!

GOLDEN CHAINSAW
Look out! This twin-bladed chainsaw is super-sharp.

Golden blade can be thrown or attached to another weapon or vehicle

Removable ZX hood

Same steely expression as original minifigure (see p.40)

Holes at back of pauldrons can hold two katana swords

New ZX robes printed on torso, with one blue arm and one gray arm

ZX obi sash printed on legs

LIGHTNING WARRIOR
Jay has trained long and hard to become a great Ninja. With his new ZX skills, Jay is faster than ever in combat. The enemy won't see that silver blade coming!

STORM FIGHTER

FIGHTING WITH LIGHTNING

THE STORM FIGHTER is Jay's super-speedy, streamlined battle jet. He can blast through the skies at top speed and then "transform" the jet to launch the Storm's wing attack function, knocking his enemies flying in all directions. Watch out, Serpents!

NINJA FILE

SET NAME	JAY'S STORM FIGHTER
SET NUMBER	9442
YEAR	2012
PIECES	242

NINJA PILOT
Jay is a skilled pilot and loves flying his jet. He is deadly fast in combat on the ground and in the sky he strikes out of the blue, just like his elemental power—Lightning. Jay's enemies are often caught by surprise.

Cockpit lid lifts up

Streamlined jet nose piece

Golden serrated blade

IN THE COCKPIT
The tinted plastic cockpit lid opens and closes to allow Jay's minifigure to be slotted into position in the pilot seat of his Storm Fighter.

MINIFIGURES
Jay must recover the Golden Fangpyre Staff and its powerful anti-venom. Snappa is not going to give it up without a fight.

Jay ZX

Snappa

Button for activating wing transformation

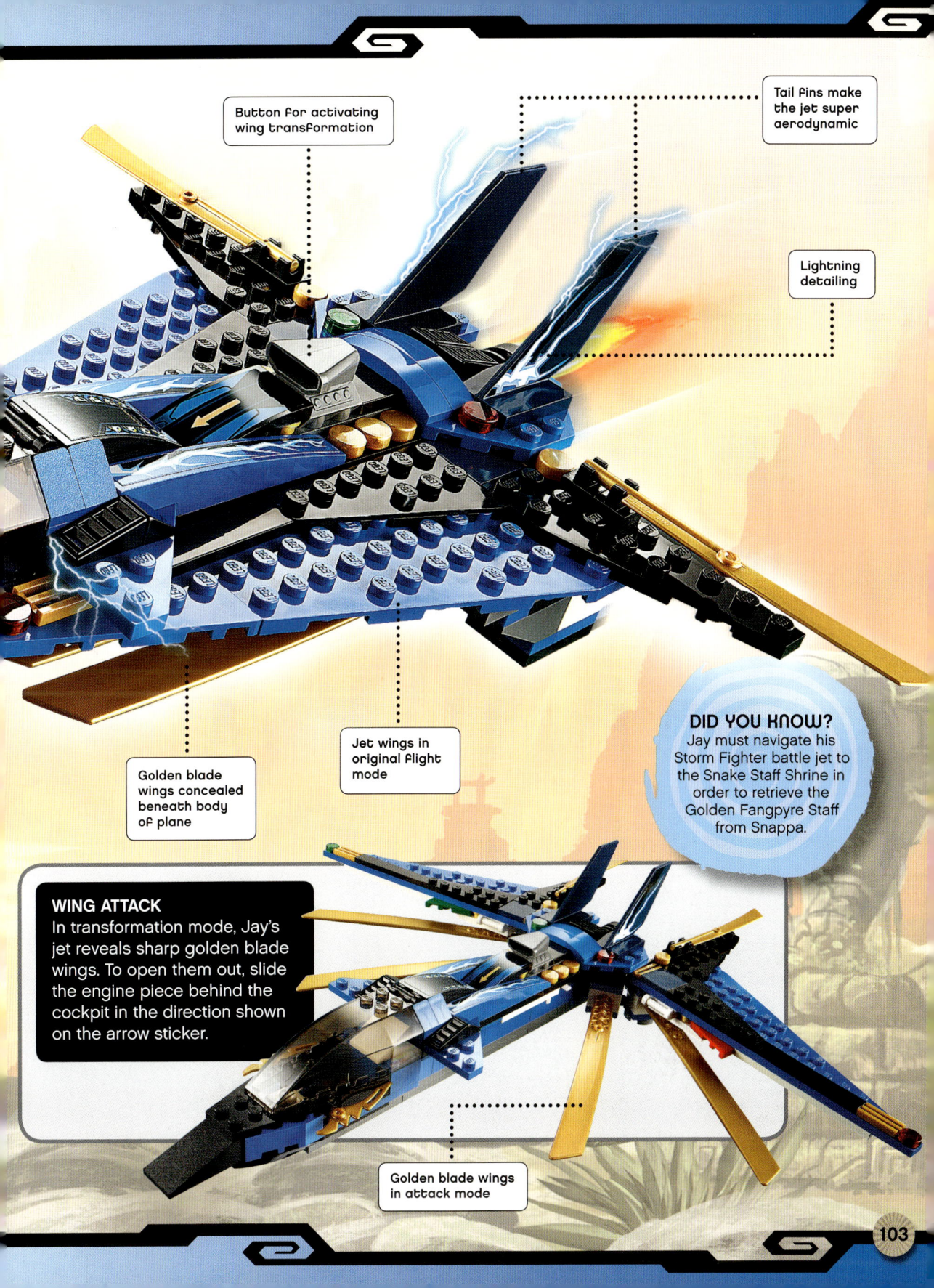

Tail fins make the jet super aerodynamic

Lightning detailing

Golden blade wings concealed beneath body of plane

Jet wings in original flight mode

DID YOU KNOW?
Jay must navigate his Storm Fighter battle jet to the Snake Staff Shrine in order to retrieve the Golden Fangpyre Staff from Snappa.

WING ATTACK
In transformation mode, Jay's jet reveals sharp golden blade wings. To open them out, slide the engine piece behind the cockpit in the direction shown on the arrow sticker.

Golden blade wings in attack mode

103

SAMURAI X
SECRET WARRIOR

WHO IS HIDING behind Samurai X's mask? For a while no one knows who this mysterious secret warrior is, but one day the truth is revealed to Jay. Samurai X is Nya, Kai's sister! Kai told her that only a Ninja could fight villains. However, Nya shows him that a Samurai (and a girl!) has what it takes to be a hero!

- Ornamental spiked Samurai crest
- Protective silver helmet
- Mask to hide identity
- Protective body armor with extended shoulder pads
- Red warrior dress robes are practical as well as stylish

DID YOU KNOW?
"Samurai" was the name given to ancient Japanese warriors. The Samurai's main weapon was the katana sword and warriors often gave their blades names.

ONE OF THE BOYS
When Samurai X reveals her identity, the Ninja are surprised. However, they see that Nya is just as brave and skilled as they are. She might even be able to teach them some things!

NINJA FILE
SET NAME	SAMURAI X
SET NUMBER	9566
YEAR	2012
PIECES	23

SAMURAI SPINNER
Nya practices hard and is a skilled sword fighter. With her super Samurai spinner she can whip up a fierce and fiery tornado.

Neckguard

New angry facial expression

Red face guard protects head

Removable armor

Fang Blade with vial of venom attached to the end of the handle

Samurai dress robe design with phoenix symbol printed on torso and legs

Samurai X crown to decorate the spinner

Phoenix symbols on spinner base

Spinner base

WEAPONS

BUTTERFLY SWORD
This weapon looks good and also helps Samurai X to fight against the Serpentine.

GOLDEN KATANA
The blade of this Samurai weapon is deadly sharp.

Sharp and fiery spear head

SPEAR OF FIRE
No one knows the true powers of Samurai X's special spear, not even Nya herself.

GIRL POWER!
Nya is smart, but the Ninja don't always listen to her. She is able to cure a Fangpyre bite and knows that getting just one Fang Blade will stop the Great Devourer being unleashed.

SAMURAI MECH
ROBOT WARS

THE SAMURAI MECH is a massive robot controlled by Samurai X. It comes equipped with a fierce arsenal of weapons—including a cannon shooter, a flick missile device, sharp claws for crushing, and a mighty sword—but will all this be enough to fend off the Serpents?

Bytar **Snike** **Samurai X**

MINIFIGURES
Rare minifigures Bytar and Snike don't stand much of a chance against the might of Samurai X's Mech.

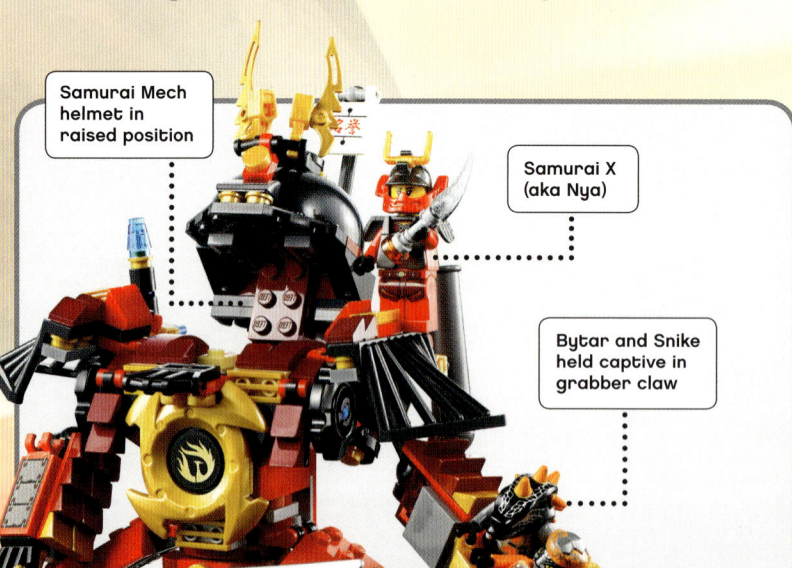

- Samurai Mech helmet in raised position
- Samurai X (aka Nya)
- Bytar and Snike held captive in grabber claw

CATAPULT AMBUSH
Snike and Bytar have a catapult to launch missiles—or themselves—at Samurai X! Flick the rod piece to launch chaos from the barrel.

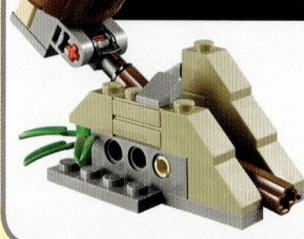

- Serpent catapult mechanism

ROBO-POWERED
The Mech's helmet lifts up to reveal Samurai X's cockpit. Its giant hands have grabber claws that open and close for grasping weapons or even minifigures.

DID YOU KNOW?
The Snike minifigure is exclusive to Samurai Mech, (set 9448), whereas Samurai X and Bytar also appear in their own spinner sets. This is the only non-spinner set to include none of the four Ninja.

ROBOT MIGHT

Samurai X, aka Nya, has adorned her powerful Mech robot with Samurai detailing to intimidate her enemies. As she maneuvers the Mech to grab the Constrictai Fang Blade, Bytar and Snike launch a catapult ambush on her and the robot.

- Samurai flag with Japanese emblems
- Samurai helmet conceals the cockpit
- Samurai X in cockpit
- Shoulder cannon shooter
- Movable grabber claws
- Giant-sized sword unique to this set
- Nya's phoenix symbol printed on robot torso, within golden spinner crown piece
- Robot feet turn, and posable legs swivel at hips

NINJA FILE

SET NAME	SAMURAI MECH
SET NUMBER	9448
YEAR	2012
PIECES	452

COLE ZX

EARTH ZEN EXTREME

THANKS TO HOURS of practice, Cole has achieved the ZX, or Zen, level of his Ninja training. The Cole ZX minifigure wears a new uniform to mark his raised status. As leader of the Ninja, it is now Cole's job to help the others develop their own Zen eXtreme skills.

New hood has silver detail

NINJA FILE

SET NAME STARTER SET
SET NUMBER 9579
YEAR 2012
PIECES 62

Ninja wrap masks face

Protective leather-style chest plate

ZX black robe, chest sash, and belt printed on torso and legs

WEAPONS

TRUSTY AX
This ax is the perfect defensive weapon. The silver color matches Cole's pauldrons.

NINJAGO SWORD
Cole's sword skills are even better now he has achieved his Zen status.

Pointed striker head

GOLDEN TRI SCYTHE
This three-pronged weapon is the ultimate Serpentine repellent.

ZX UNIFORM
As a ZX Ninja, Cole wears silver shoulder pauldrons to protect his upper body. The back of the pauldrons form a circular holder, where Cole keeps his katana sword.

108

ZX SPINNER

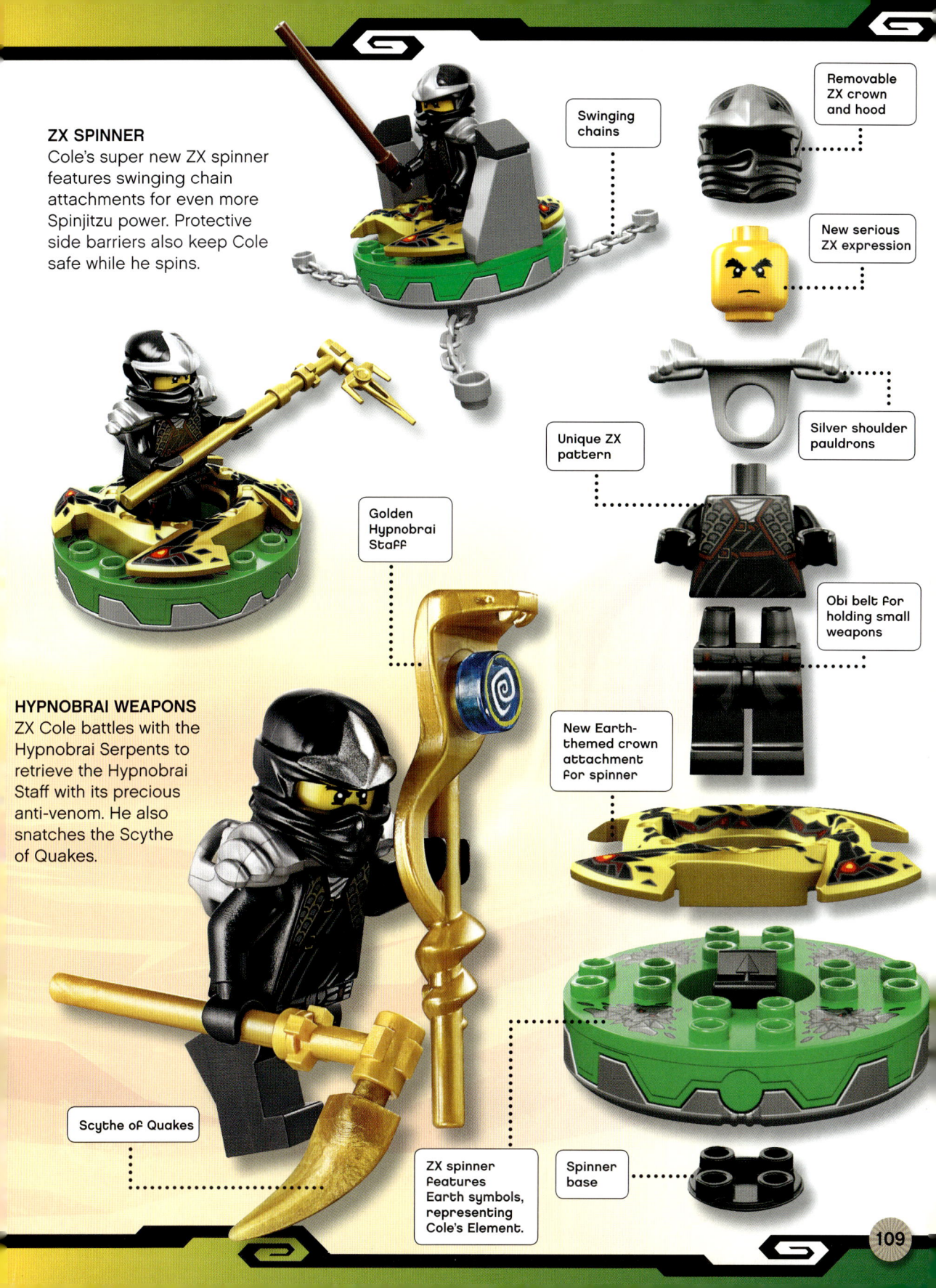

Cole's super new ZX spinner features swinging chain attachments for even more Spinjitzu power. Protective side barriers also keep Cole safe while he spins.

HYPNOBRAI WEAPONS

ZX Cole battles with the Hypnobrai Serpents to retrieve the Hypnobrai Staff with its precious anti-venom. He also snatches the Scythe of Quakes.

- Swinging chains
- Removable ZX crown and hood
- New serious ZX expression
- Unique ZX pattern
- Silver shoulder pauldrons
- Golden Hypnobrai Staff
- Obi belt for holding small weapons
- New Earth-themed crown attachment for spinner
- Scythe of Quakes
- ZX spinner features Earth symbols, representing Cole's Element.
- Spinner base

TREAD ASSAULT

SERPENTS BEWARE!

THIS FOUR-WHEELED vehicle is tough enough to take on the evil leader of the Hypnobrai tribe, General Skales! Driven by Cole, it is armed with a rocket missile launcher and six terrifying Ninja blades. It also has a secret camouflage mode for surprise attacks. Watch out, General Skales, Cole is coming to get you!

NINJA FILE

SET NAME	COLE'S TREAD ASSAULT
SET NUMBER	9444
YEAR	2012
PIECES	286

SLIPPERY ENEMY
Cole hopes that this powerful assault vehicle will help him defeat General Skales and reclaim the Hypnobrai Staff. However, Skales has a few tricks of his own, including some evil mind control powers.

MINIFIGURES
Cole must stop Skales escaping with the Hypnobrai Staff. Luckily, his assault vehicle is fast!

Skales

Cole ZX

Rocket missile can be fired at enemies.

Rocket shooter

Two golden daggers provide extra piercing action.

Two golden katana swords at front of vehicle

SNAKE DISGUISE
Cole's Tread Assault vehicle has a clever camouflage device for sneaking into Serpentine territory. When it is flipped over, green Serpentine-styling is revealed—Cole can even drive it in this position!

Green elements make vehicle look Serpentine!

Cockpit flips around

Black and gold design mirrors Cole's costume

One of six movable blades

Mechanism to flip out Ninja blades located beneath engine

All-terrain tire

Tread Assault vehicle in original mode

111

ZANE ZX

ICE ZEN EXTREME

ZANE IS NOW an expert ZX, or Zen eXtreme, Ninja. His ZX minifigure features gold pauldrons and gold detailing on his hood to reflect his new status. Zane's mastery of the Element of Ice has also reached an even higher level.

New hood has built-in crown

Katana sword fits into circular holder on back

Ridged gold shoulder pauldrons

New robes feature entwined rope belts and plain white undershirt

NINJA FILE

- SET NAME ZANE ZX
- SET NUMBER 9554
- YEAR 2012
- PIECES 37

DID YOU KNOW?
Zane is a robot. His father, Dr. Julien, turned Zane's memory switch (located in a hidden panel in his chest) off, so that Zane wouldn't know he was a robot and could therefore lead a normal life.

TWO KATANA
Zane is a stealthy Ninja and a brave warrior. Thanks to his new ZX outfit, he can carry two katana swords on his back. This means he can fight more than one Serpent at once. NINJA-GO!

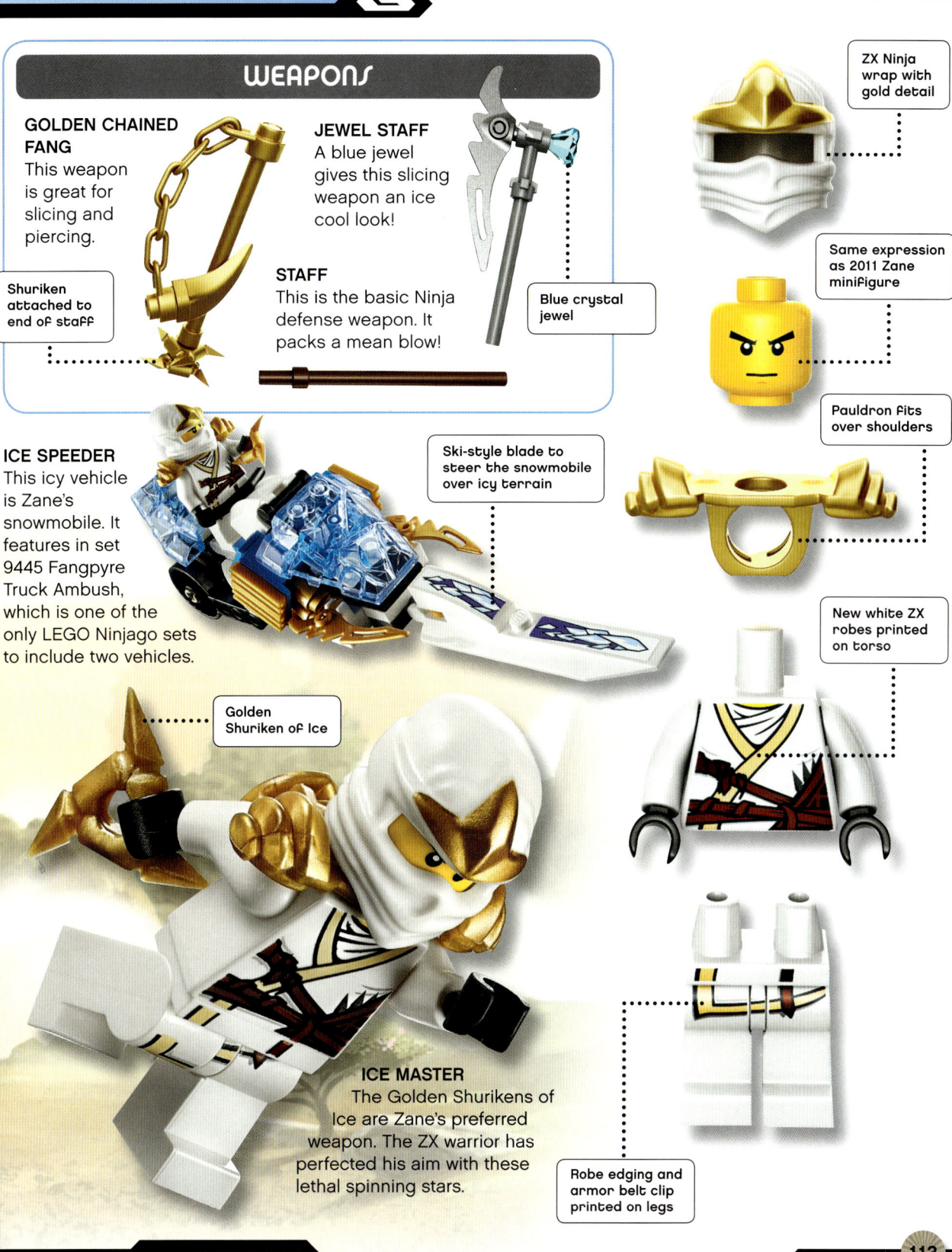

WEAPONS

GOLDEN CHAINED FANG
This weapon is great for slicing and piercing.

Shuriken attached to end of staff

JEWEL STAFF
A blue jewel gives this slicing weapon an ice cool look!

STAFF
This is the basic Ninja defense weapon. It packs a mean blow!

Blue crystal jewel

ZX Ninja wrap with gold detail

Same expression as 2011 Zane minifigure

Pauldron fits over shoulders

ICE SPEEDER
This icy vehicle is Zane's snowmobile. It features in set 9445 Fangpyre Truck Ambush, which is one of the only LEGO Ninjago sets to include two vehicles.

Ski-style blade to steer the snowmobile over icy terrain

New white ZX robes printed on torso

Golden Shuriken of Ice

ICE MASTER
The Golden Shurikens of Ice are Zane's preferred weapon. The ZX warrior has perfected his aim with these lethal spinning stars.

Robe edging and armor belt clip printed on legs

113

ULTRA SONIC RAIDER

TORNADO OF CREATION

THIS AWESOME SONIC vehicle is made from recycled scrap vehicles. It was created when the four Ninja used Spinjitzu to combine their four elemental tornadoes into the Tornado of Creation. With its dual tank/aircraft modes and multiple weapon functions, the Raider is the ultimate multipurpose fighting machine!

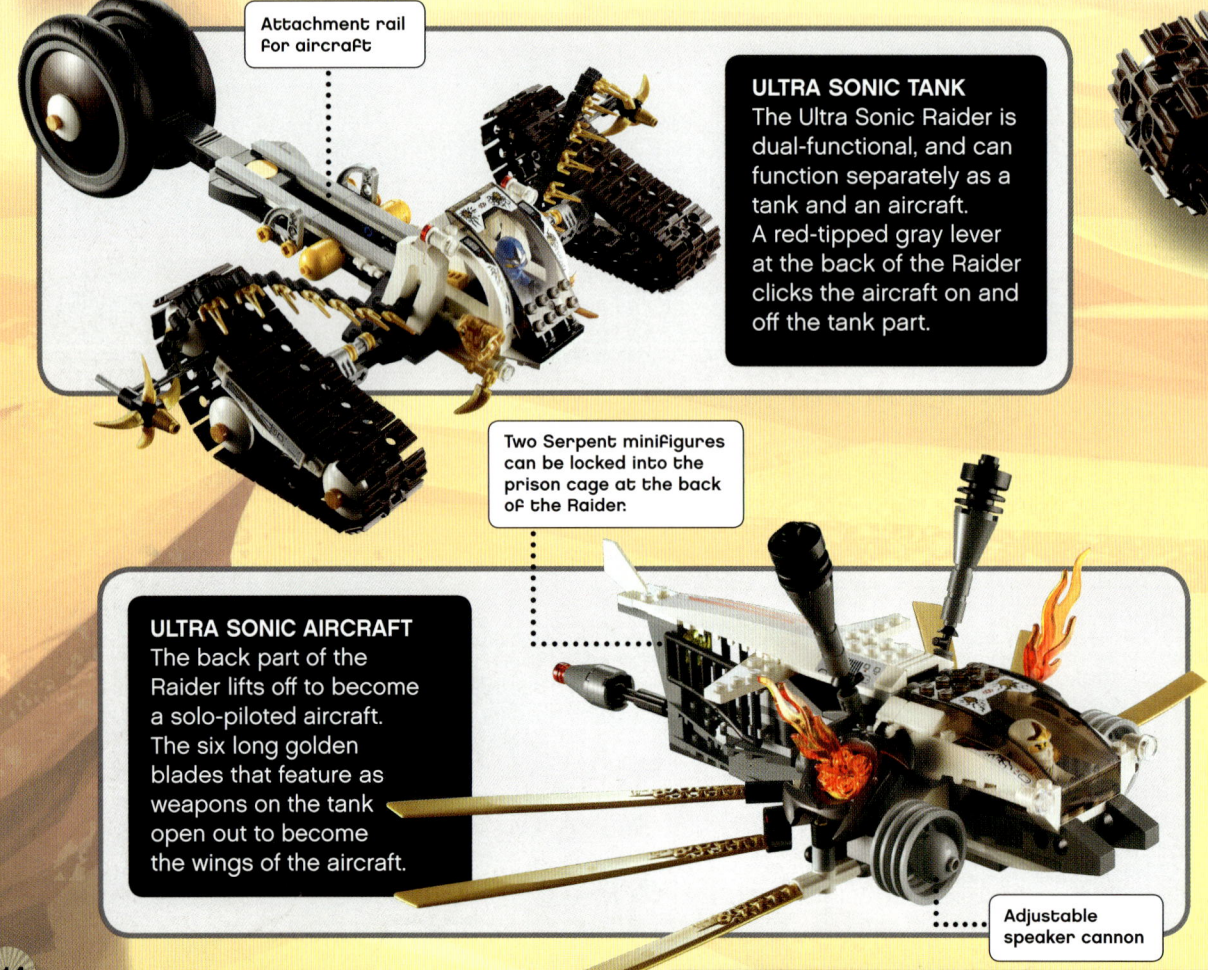

NINJA FILE
- **SET NAME** ULTRA SONIC RAIDER
- **SET NUMBER** 9449
- **YEAR** 2012
- **PIECES** 622

Attachment rail for aircraft

ULTRA SONIC TANK
The Ultra Sonic Raider is dual-functional, and can function separately as a tank and an aircraft. A red-tipped gray lever at the back of the Raider clicks the aircraft on and off the tank part.

Two Serpent minifigures can be locked into the prison cage at the back of the Raider.

ULTRA SONIC AIRCRAFT
The back part of the Raider lifts off to become a solo-piloted aircraft. The six long golden blades that feature as weapons on the tank open out to become the wings of the aircraft.

Adjustable speaker cannon

MINIFIGURES
United for the first time in one set, the four Ninja must battle the snakes and travel to Ninjago City in the Raider to destroy the Great Devourer.

Spitta | Pythor | Jay ZX | Kai ZX | Cole ZX | Zane ZX

Each cockpit can hold one minifigure.

Flame pieces fit into spinner crown pieces attached to the side of the tank.

Large double wheel to help steer the tank

Golden blades become wings when the Raider is in aircraft mode

A row of 8 golden sai daggers slots on to each side of the front of the tank.

Golden Weapon of Spinjitzu

Unique brown tire treads

Dagger flick missile—one on each side of the tank

SACRED MUSIC
The Serpents and the Great Devourer can be controlled by sacred flute music. Zane installs recordings of this music into the speaker cannon on the Raider, as a secret weapon.

KAI

Sword-fighting is an important part of Kendo. Fortunately, Kai is already an expert with his elemental Weapon, the Dragon Sword of Fire. Kendo is no problem for Kai!

KENDO NINJA

THE NINJA ARE always ready to learn new skills to give them an edge over their enemies. When Sensei Wu teaches them the complex martial art called Kendo, they have to train very hard to master this Samurai style of fighting. To be Kendo Ninja they must reach a higher level of physical agility and mental control. Have they got what it takes? Of course they have!

COLE

Kendo can be a very dangerous style of fighting, so the Ninja must wear armor. Cole has a protective helmet, mask, and body armor.

ZANE

Zane is the Ninja of Ice, but in his Kendo outfit he looks more like an ice hockey player. Zane just thinks he looks cool…

JAY

Once they have mastered Kendo, the Ninja can use any weapons they like. Jay chooses the dark talons and a golden blade.

NRG NINJA

EACH TIME A Ninja reaches the next level he gains a new status and a stylish new outfit. First, they become DX (Dragon eXtreme), then ZX (Zen eXtreme), then Kendo, and finally, when they reach their full potential, they become NRG Ninja. Each individual Ninja's full potential means something different, but for every one of them it means finding out who they really are.

JAY
A kiss from Kai's sister Nya unlocks Jay's full potential. His NRG outfit features an eye-catching new Lightning design.

KAI
Kai is the last to become an NRG Ninja. To progress to the highest level Kai must finally learn to control his fiery temper.

ZANE
Zane is the first Ninja to realize his full potential. For him it means learning that he is really a robot, and accepting that fact.

COLE
Leader Cole is the third Ninja to find his full potential. His NRG outfit is much brighter than his other ones—it is black and pink!

THE GREEN NINJA

MASTER OF ALL ELEMENTS

AN ANCIENT PROPHECY foretold that a Green Ninja would rise above all other Ninja, to fight the darkness. And here he is! The Green Ninja possesses the power of the four main Elements—Earth, Lightning, Ice, and Fire.

NINJA FILE

- **SET NAME** EPIC DRAGON BATTLE
- **SET NUMBER** 9450
- **YEAR** 2012
- **PIECES** 915

Lloyd's identity is hidden by his green wrap.

Detachable protective shoulder and back armor

Pale shirt worn beneath special Green Ninja robe

Unique silver belt clasp

WEAPONS

SUPER BOLT
Only the Green Ninja has this golden weapon, with its unique green blades.

SILVER SWORD
All Ninja are skilled in the art of sword fighting. The katana is the best sword to use in combat.

NIN-JÔ STAFF
A simple but classic weapon, this staff is effective in the hands of a trained Ninja.

NOT-SO-BAD
The Green Ninja's identity is revealed to be Lloyd Garmadon. He is not such a bad boy after all! When he went near the four Golden Weapons, a green aura appeared around him and he became the Green Ninja.

POWER OF THE ELEMENTS

On his super spinner and with his magical super bolt weapon, the Green Ninja can spin up the most terrifying and powerful tornado. Watch out, Serpents (and Dad)!

EXCLUSIVE ZX NINJA

This exclusive minifigure is only available with the trade edition of this book. It represents the Green Ninja with ZX status. He has a new black and green uniform with gold decoration.

- Green Ninja wrap with silver crown
- Face piece reveals Green Ninja to be Lloyd Garmadon (see also p.126)!
- Shoulder armor and weapon carrier
- Silver detail printed on torso
- Diamond pattern continues on legs
- Unique Green Ninja crown fits to spinner
- Horns fit to spinner for extra bashing power
- Gold spinner with symbols of all four Elements
- Golden Serpents fit to spinner to send opponents tumbling

- Exclusive gold detail on headwrap
- Gold pauldrons
- Decorative black, green, and gold robe
- Traditional obi Ninja sash

119

MEET THE SERPENTINE

COME AND MEET the five Serpentine tribes—if you dare. Many years ago the Serpentine ruled Ninjago with the Great Devourer, but they were driven out and sealed into five separate tombs. Now, thanks to little Lloyd Garmadon, they're back! Each tribe has different markings, powers, and weapons, but they all have one thing in common—they are evil.

DID YOU KNOW? The Hypnobrai, Fangpyre, Venomari, and Constrictai tribes each have their own Golden Staff. These weapons contain a vial of anti-venom—the only antidote to the Serpents' vile venom!

SNAKE TRIBES:

ANACONDRAI These purple snakes were the largest of the tribes, but only one remains. His jaws are big enough to swallow a person whole.

HYPNOBRAI These blue, cobra-like snakes have powerful, hypnotic eyes.

FANGPYRE These red Serpents turn their foes into snakes with one bite. They make vehicles for the other tribes.

VENOMARI A bite from these green four-eyed fiends causes victims to hallucinate (imagine things).

CONSTRICTAI These heavy orange and black Serpents live underground. They kill their enemies by crushing them.

ANACONDRAI

PYTHOR

The Anacondrai didn't have any food in their tomb so they all got very hungry. Desperate, they all started eating each other until only General Pythor remained. He is now the supreme leader of all the Serpents. He is purple, poisonous, and perfectly horrible!

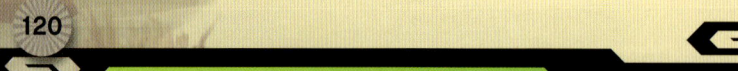

HYPNOBRAI

SKALES

General Skales is the leader of the Hypnobrai tribe but wants even more power! He is a master of the ancient martial art Fang-kwon-do.

MEZMO

This soldier is always happy to carry out General Skales's orders. Mezmo has the hypnotic red eyes and sharp fangs that are common to all Hypnobrai.

SLITHRAA

This warrior was his tribe's general, before Skales. Slithraa once tried to hypnotize Lloyd Garmadon but it backfired and he hypnotized himself instead!

RATTLA

Rattla is not the sharpest Serpent in the tribe, but he is happy to go along with whatever Skales tells him to do. He also has a secret passion for singing!

FANGPYRE

FANGDAM

Second-in-command of the Fangpyre tribe, Fangdam has two heads but can't speak from either of them.

SNAPPA

This fiery Fangpyre is his tribe's scout and sniper, which means he is great at finding—and catching—foes.

ACIDICUS

General Acidicus is the brains of the Venomari tribe—but that is not saying much! He makes sure that the tribe never runs out of venom.

FANG-SUEI

Fang-Suei is so strong and tough that he can use a banana as a weapon! Don't mess with this slippery Serpent.

FANGTOM

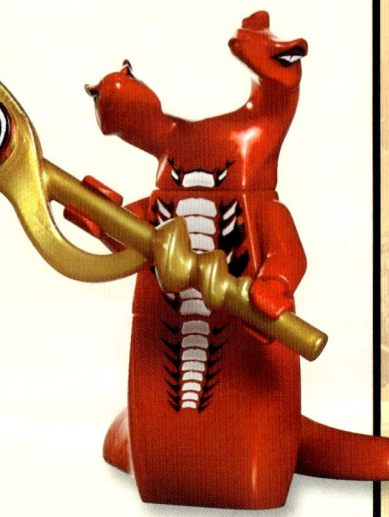

Two heads are definitely better than one for Fangpyre General Fangtom. His heads like to finish each other's sentences!

LASHA

Despite his missing eye, Lasha is the Venomari's chief scout. With his good eye, he has no problem spotting the enemy.

VENOMARI

LIZARU

This four-fanged Venomari is a fearsome warrior. He likes to help Acidicus plan their battles against the Ninja.

SPITTA

Spitta's teeth are so large that he can't close his mouth. That means all his venom leaks out and he can sell it to the other Venomari.

CONSTRICTAI

BYTAR

This Constrictai warrior has plenty of muscles, but not much height. His favorite things are fighting, eating, and sleeping.

SKALIDOR

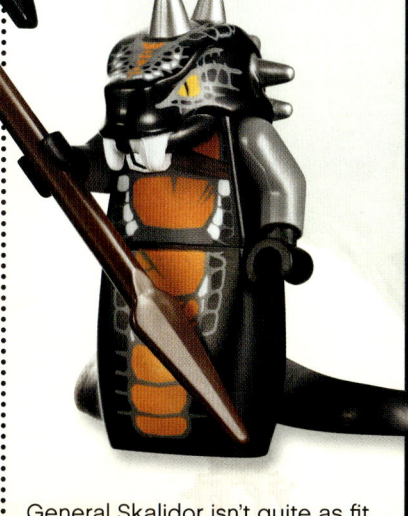

General Skalidor isn't quite as fit and muscular as the rest of his tribe, but if anyone attacks him he can always sit on them!

SNIKE

Snike is the Constrictai's sniper. Unfortunately he is color-blind and cross-eyed! However, he still hits the target—most of the time.

CHOKUN

Chokun is pretty small for a Serpent. But what he lacks for in height and muscle, he makes up for in fang size.

123

THE NINJA ARE HISSSSTORY!

TO SLITHER LIKE A SERPENTINE YOU MUST:

MASTER YOUR TRIBE'S SPECIAL POWER

BE VICIOUS, CUNNING, AND SNEAKY

KEEP YOUR FANGS SHARPENED

ALWAYS OBEY YOUR GENERAL

LORD GARMADON

THE RETURN

HE'S BACK! HAVING returned from the Underworld, Lord Garmadon still wants to take over Ninjago, and also wants revenge on the Ninja for thwarting his evil plans. This time he is stronger than ever with a double torso and four arms! However, he is also a father, and his love for his son might just make him a better person…

NINJA FILE
SET NAME	EPIC DRAGON BATTLE
SET NUMBER	9450
YEAR	2012
PIECES	915

DID YOU KNOW? The new version of Garmadon's minifigure is made up of the same head and body as his 2011 minifigure (see p.50), with an extra upper body piece to hold two additional arms!

- Nunchucks of Lightning
- Sword of Fire
- Scythe of Quakes
- Removable second torso with two extra arms
- Shuriken of Ice

FOUR ARMS
Thanks to his four arms, Lord Garmadon can now control all four Golden Weapons of Spinjitzu. He is a formidable opponent but he will help an enemy if it means saving his beloved son, Lloyd.

LLOYD GARMADON

SON OF LORD GARMADON

LLOYD IS NOT quite as bad as his father, Lord Garmadon. Young Lloyd attends Darkley's Boarding School for Bad Boys and is more interested in candy and practical jokes than plotting to take over Ninjago.

NINJA FILE
- **SET NAME** LLOYD GARMADON
- **SET NUMBER** 9552
- **YEAR** 2012
- **PIECES** 26

WEAPONS

SPEAR OF FORKED-TONGUES
Each tongue is filled with venom, ready to be injected into enemies.

GOLDEN VIPER
A small but lethal poisonous snake.

BLINDING STAFF
Shine the light in the enemies eyes to blind them.

SNAKE CHARMER
Lloyd accidentally releases all the Serpent tribes and becomes their leader. He orders the Serpents to do childish things such as steal candy. The snakes are not impressed and soon betray him. Fortunately, his Uncle Wu and the Ninja come to his rescue.

- Black hooded cloak is removable
- Cheeky expression
- Sports-style top mixed with hand-painted skeleton design
- Lloyd is still a child, so his minifigure has short, unposable legs.

VENOMARI SHRINE

SNAKE STAFF BATTLE

ZANE MUST USE his Ninja skills to retrieve the Golden Venomari Staff and the anti-venom hidden inside it. Can he avoid the snake fangs, slime, and acid spit in the Shrine and escape with the Staff?

NINJA FILE
- **SET NAME** VENOMARI SHRINE
- **SET NUMBER** 9440
- **YEAR** 2012
- **PIECES** 86

MINIFIGURES
Zane is attacked by poisonous vipers as he enters the Venomari Shrine alone. He must retrieve the Golden Staff with its anti-venom to save himself.

Zane ZX

Black plank viper launch pad

ATTACK!
Flick down the black tiled planks at the back of the Shrine to launch the poisonous green vipers. Watch them fly through the air towards the Ninja intruder!

Lime green snake venom

GOLDEN VENOMARI STAFF
The centerpiece of the Shrine is a large Serpent statue. Two long fangs filled with venom drip down to the floor and the Golden Staff hangs in front of them.

DID YOU KNOW?
The Venomari Staff is one of the four Serpent Staffs which are key elements in producing a map that will lead to the discovery of the four Fang Blades. Whoever has the four Fang Blades can unleash the Great Devourer.

- Vipers can be launched at intruders.
- Snake head statue at top of Shrine
- Golden Venomari Staff with vial of anti-venom

TOXIC VENOM
The Venomari tribe's toxic venom causes terrible hallucinations in its victims. The General of the tribe, Acidicus, carries the Golden Venomari Staff, which contains a vial of anti-venom—the antidote to their own toxic venom!

- Realistic LEGO brick design is new for this set.
- Dripping venom
- Viper ready to be launched

ACIDICUS
VENOMARI GENERAL

NINJA FILE
SET NAME	EPIC DRAGON BATTLE
SET NUMBER	9450
YEAR	2012
PIECES	915

Two rows of head spikes

Acidicus has two scars behind his left back eye.

Acidicus has two side fangs as well as two front fangs.

Vial of anti-venom clips onto end of Hypnobrai Fang Blade handle

Distinctive green and orange scale pattern

All Serpent Generals have a snake tail instead of legs.

GENERAL OF the Venomari Army, Acidicus is clever and crafty. He has constructed vials that the Venomari use to carry extra venom in their combat gear, so they never run out of poison in battle. How brilliantly evil!

FANG BLADES
Acidicus usually wields the Venomari Fang Blade, but here he's got the Hypnobrai one. There are four ancient silver Fang Blades for each of the four tribes (Venomari, Hypnobrai, Fangpyre, and Constrictai). Whoever holds all four Blades can unleash the Serpentine beast, the Great Devourer.

SPITTA
VENOMARI WARRIOR

THIS VENOMARI warrior's fangs are so large that his mouth is permanently open. Because of this, he drools a lot, leaking venom wherever he goes. Yuck—how slimy!

NINJA FILE

SET NAME	SPITTA
SET NUMBER	9569
YEAR	2012
PIECES	20

WEAPONS

VENOM PICKAX
The venom vial makes this weapon even more lethal.

PURPLE VIPER
This purple snake is small but dangerous and highly toxic.

SCYTHE BLADE
This big, heavy, slicing blade is great for cutting down large enemies.

- Unique head markings
- Four yellow eyes are a feature of all Venomari snakes.
- Over-sized fangs, unique to Spitta
- Light green scale pattern and scars printed on torso
- Vials of venom carried in shoulder belt

VENOM SUPPLIER
Spitta uses the vials invented by Acidicus to store his excess venom. He sells it to the other snakes in his tribe, for times when they can't produce enough venom of their own.

131

LASHA
VENOMARI SCOUT

LASHA IS THE best scout in the Venomari tribe, despite the fact that he has lost an eye. He keeps a lookout for enemies and seeks out prey for the rest of the Venomari to attack. Watch out, Ninja! Lasha is mean and isn't scared of anything.

NINJA FILE
- **SET NAME** LASHA
- **SET NUMBER** 9562
- **YEAR** 2012
- **PIECES** 21

WEAPONS

TOXIC VIPER
This tiny viper is highly poisonous and its bite causes hallucinations.

GOLDEN AX
The perfect Serpentine weapon. One swing will knock the enemy back.

CHAINED FANG OF POISON
The green vial can be filled with venom and the piercing fang can be swung at the enemy.

Vial of venom

- Distinctive cobra hood, opened wide to intimidate enemies
- Missing eye was lost in battle
- Serpentine forked tongue
- Bandolier shoulder belt for holding vials
- Red vial for storing extra venom

SMALL FANGS
Lasha's fangs are too small to produce much venom of his own. He has to buy extra venom so that he has enough to use on his enemies. His fangs hurt most of the time because he ate too much candy when he was a young Serpent.

POISONOUS SPINNER

The Serpentine tribes are also masters of Spinjitzu. The combination of toxic venom, lethal weapons, and the power of Spinjitzu is truly frightening!

DID YOU KNOW? Lasha's minifigure wears the same cobra headpiece as Rattla (p.153), although they are decorated and colored differently—Lasha's is lime green, whereas Rattla's is white.

- Removable cobra hood headpiece
- Face piece unique to Lasha's minifigure
- Scarred torso
- Bright green legs show Lasha is not a General.
- Green toxic viper snake
- Serpent spinner crown attachment
- Slot Serpent into place to take on the Ninja!
- Venomari symbol
- Spinner base

TOXIC VIPER

The green viper may be small, but this highly toxic creature causes its victims to hallucinate and develop really bad breath. Eeek! Don't get too close...

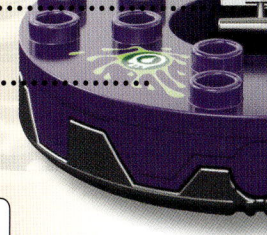

133

LASHA'S BITE CYCLE

FANG BLADE THEFT

WHILE EXAMINING ONE of the long-lost Fang Blades in the Blacksmith's Forge, Cole is paid a surprise visit! Lasha zooms past on his slick Bite Cycle and seizes the Blade. Luckily for Lasha, the Bite Cycle is ideal for carrying out a stealth attack—it is lightning-fast, and the Serpent makes a quick getaway...

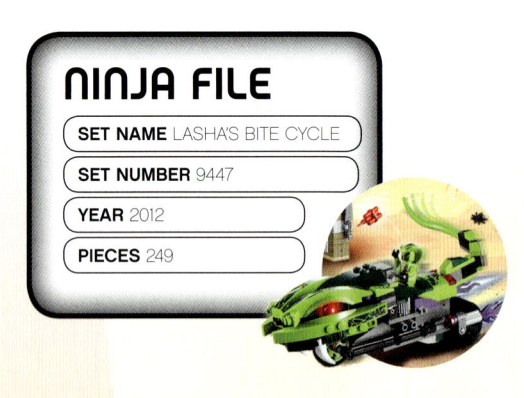

NINJA FILE
- **SET NAME** LASHA'S BITE CYCLE
- **SET NUMBER** 9447
- **YEAR** 2012
- **PIECES** 249

- Pillar rack for storing weapons
- Blacksmith's workbench
- Fire for forging weapons
- Giant snake head is hinged and moves menacingly up and down
- Red balls add evil snake eyes feature
- Large fangs for biting the enemy

BLACKSMITH'S FORGE
This mini blacksmith's workshop features exclusively in this set and comes equipped with a forging fire, a workbench, a weapons rack, four regular weapons, and an anvil hammer.

SCOUTING MISSION

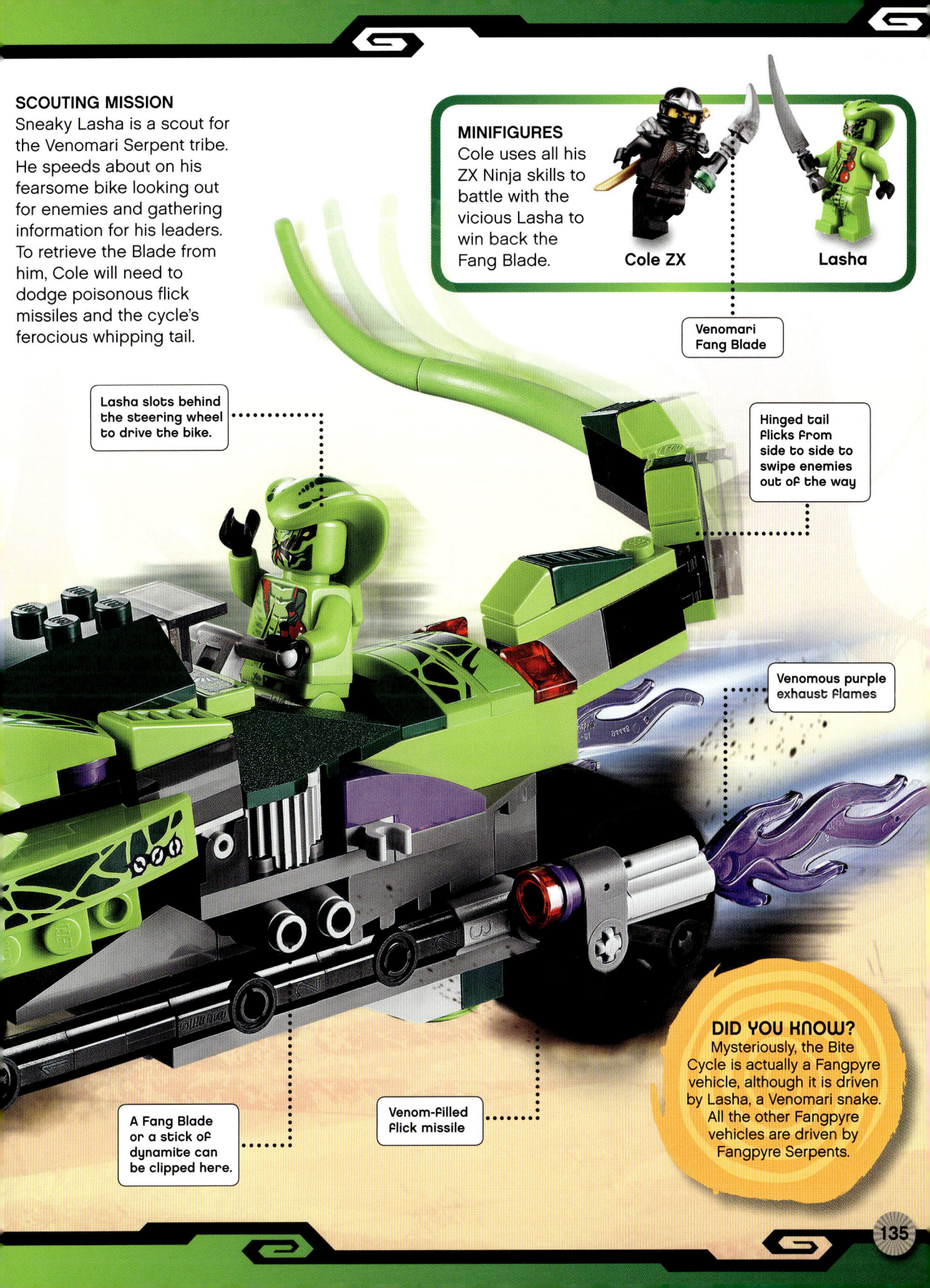

Sneaky Lasha is a scout for the Venomari Serpent tribe. He speeds about on his fearsome bike looking out for enemies and gathering information for his leaders. To retrieve the Blade from him, Cole will need to dodge poisonous flick missiles and the cycle's ferocious whipping tail.

MINIFIGURES
Cole uses all his ZX Ninja skills to battle with the vicious Lasha to win back the Fang Blade.

Cole ZX

Lasha

Venomari Fang Blade

Lasha slots behind the steering wheel to drive the bike.

Hinged tail flicks from side to side to swipe enemies out of the way

Venomous purple exhaust flames

A Fang Blade or a stick of dynamite can be clipped here.

Venom-filled flick missile

DID YOU KNOW?
Mysteriously, the Bite Cycle is actually a Fangpyre vehicle, although it is driven by Lasha, a Venomari snake. All the other Fangpyre vehicles are driven by Fangpyre Serpents.

135

LIZARU

VENOMARI WARRIOR

THIS FOUR-FANGED warrior is second-in-command to Acidicus in the Venomari tribe. In his spare time he runs a potion-making business, to make lethal venoms for the Serpents.

- Distinctive striped head markings
- Two rows of head spikes
- Sinister yellow eyes
- Four fangs filled with venom
- Scaly, scarred torso similar to other members of the Venomari tribe

NINJA FILE
SET NAME	LIZARU
SET NUMBER	9557
YEAR	2012
PIECES	25

WEAPONS

AX
Simple and hefty, this ax is ideal for hacking through enemy troops.

BATTLE MACE
This swinging spiked ball could knock a minifigure into seven pieces!

DOUBLE-SIDED AX
This weapon has a fierce, double slicing action.

SCHEMING SERPENT
Lizaru can survive days or even weeks without food. He doesn't mind—it gives him time to think up terrifying schemes and make evil battle plans.

FANGTOM

FANGPYRE GENERAL

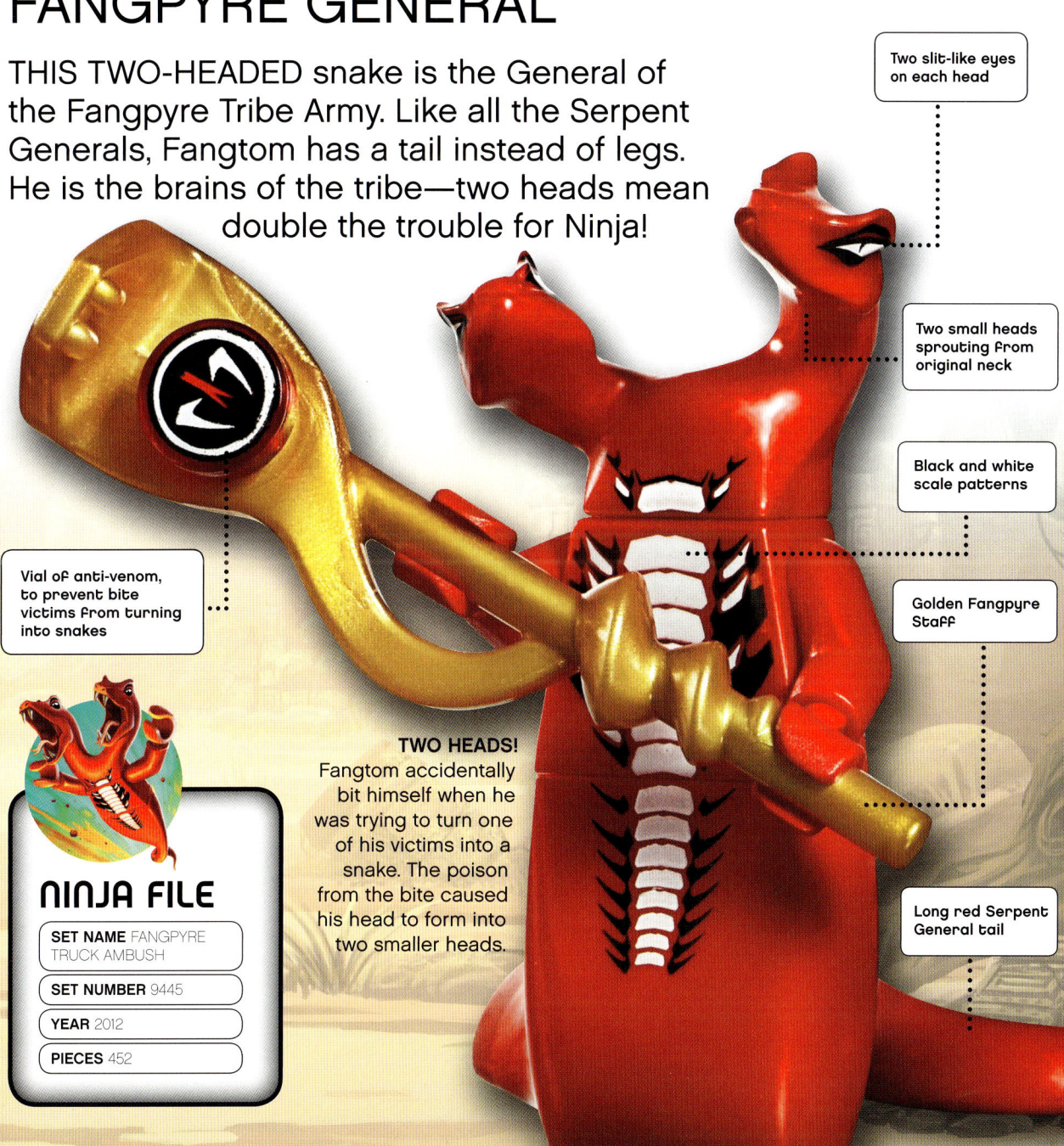

THIS TWO-HEADED snake is the General of the Fangpyre Tribe Army. Like all the Serpent Generals, Fangtom has a tail instead of legs. He is the brains of the tribe—two heads mean double the trouble for Ninja!

Two slit-like eyes on each head

Two small heads sprouting from original neck

Black and white scale patterns

Golden Fangpyre Staff

Long red Serpent General tail

Vial of anti-venom, to prevent bite victims from turning into snakes

TWO HEADS! Fangtom accidentally bit himself when he was trying to turn one of his victims into a snake. The poison from the bite caused his head to form into two smaller heads.

NINJA FILE

SET NAME	FANGPYRE TRUCK AMBUSH
SET NUMBER	9445
YEAR	2012
PIECES	452

FANGDAM

FANGPYRE WARRIOR

FANGDAM IS A warrior and second-in-command of the Fangpyre tribe. Fellow Serpent Fang-Suei once mistook him for a desert slug and bit him. The bite made him grow another head. Fangdam is fast, ferocious, and looks familiar...

WEAPONS

SLY VIPER
This white snake is a small but vicious and poisonous viper, used by Serpents in battle.

GOLDEN STAFF OF CONTROL
This staff combines the power of all the user's weapons into one super mind-controlling weapon.

Golden bi-horned fang blades

SILVER BATTLE MACE
This heavy swinging mace will knock down any enemy.

- Double-headed head piece identical to that of his brother, Fangtom
- Distinctive snake markings printed on neck
- Fangpyre scale pattern continues onto legs

DOUBLE-HEAD
Even though he has two heads, Fangdam can't speak out of either of them. Instead, he just hisses and makes a lot of noise to get himself noticed. Snappa (p.150) is the only other Fangpyre who cannot talk.

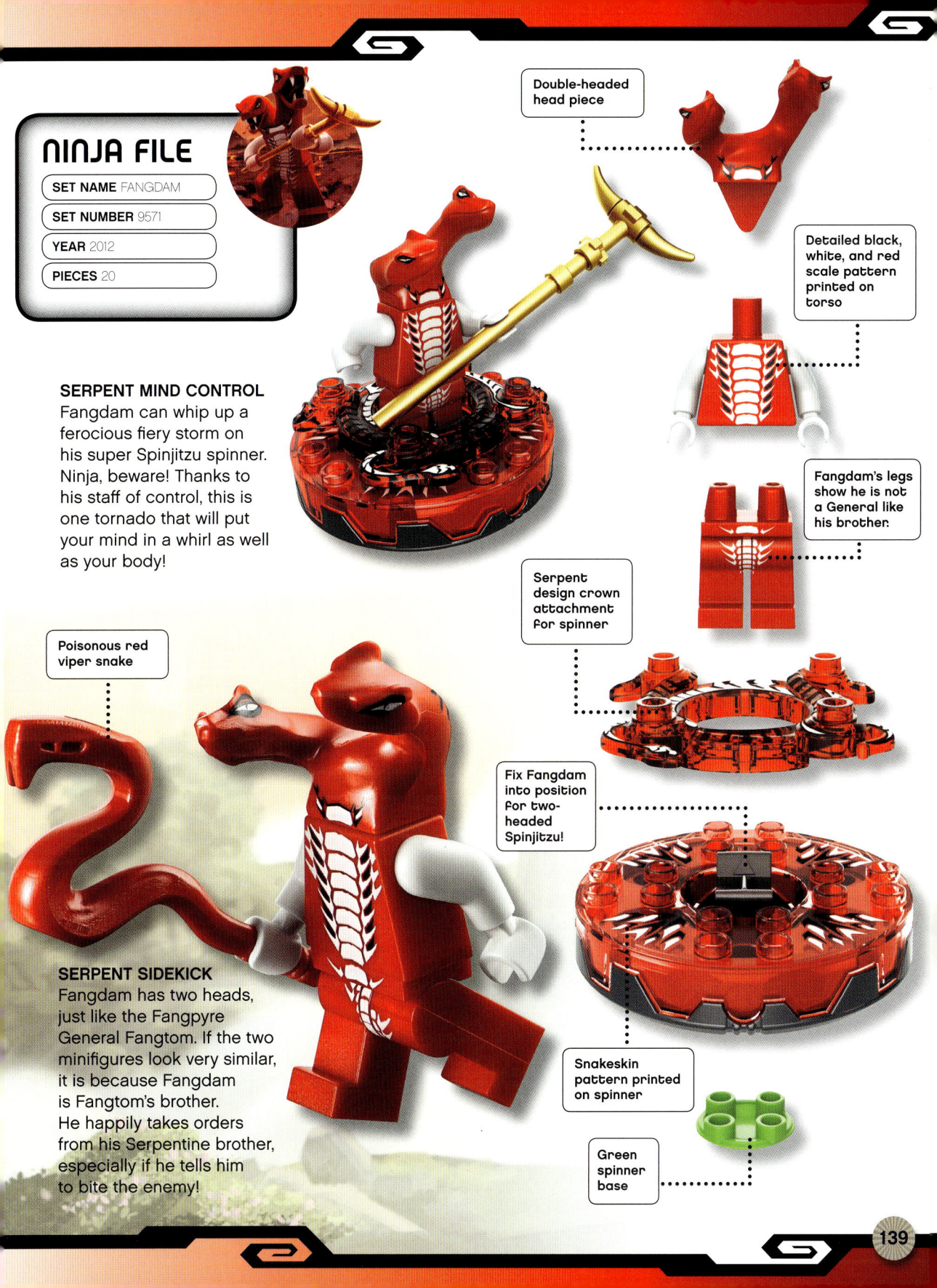

NINJA FILE

SET NAME	FANGDAM
SET NUMBER	9571
YEAR	2012
PIECES	20

SERPENT MIND CONTROL
Fangdam can whip up a ferocious fiery storm on his super Spinjitzu spinner. Ninja, beware! Thanks to his staff of control, this is one tornado that will put your mind in a whirl as well as your body!

SERPENT SIDEKICK
Fangdam has two heads, just like the Fangpyre General Fangtom. If the two minifigures look very similar, it is because Fangdam is Fangtom's brother. He happily takes orders from his Serpentine brother, especially if he tells him to bite the enemy!

Double-headed head piece

Detailed black, white, and red scale pattern printed on torso

Fangdam's legs show he is not a General like his brother.

Serpent design crown attachment for spinner

Fix Fangdam into position for two-headed Spinjitzu!

Poisonous red viper snake

Snakeskin pattern printed on spinner

Green spinner base

139

FANGPYRE TRUCK

SERPENT AMBUSH!

ZANE AND JAY have been ambushed by the slippery brothers Fangtom and Fangdam. The dangerous duo are driving their ferocious Fangpyre Truck, and its giant snake head—with opening and closing jaw—can eat Ninja if it catches them! Slot the minifigure inside the jaw and clamp it shut. Gulp! Bye, bye, Ninja!

NINJA FILE
- **SET NAME** FANGPYRE TRUCK AMBUSH
- **SET NUMBER** 9445
- **YEAR** 2011
- **PIECES** 452

TAIL END
The Fangpyre Truck's long, segmented tail can be whipped from side to side to knock over the enemy. Turn the black cog to get maximum whipping movement.

Jointed tail pieces link together

Poisonous exhaust flames

Oversized gas-fed tubing

Lethal pointed fangs

Forked tongue flicks up and down—ssssss!

Evil snake eyes made from two red balls

DINNERTIME!
The Ninja can't leave without the Fangpyre Staff and its precious anti-venom, but the Truck's whipping tail is stopping them from getting close. Can they out-run the Fangpyre Truck before its snapping fanged jaws eat them for dinner?

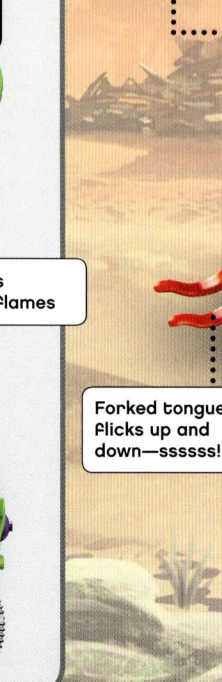

The movable segmented tail parts end in a sharp, whip-like point.

MINIFIGURES
Can the two Ninja use Zane's ice scooter to escape the vicious Fangpyre Truck?

Jay ZX   Zane ZX   Fangdam   Fangtom

Serpent driver protected by cockpit lid

Tail movement cog mechanism

HIDDEN DYNAMITE
The Fangpyre Truck has two secret weapon compartments, one on each side. The sneaky Serpents have hidden explosive dynamite inside.

Dynamite stick

Truck decorated with snakeskin patterns

Secret weapon compartment

Four large wheels complete with high-impact suspension

141

FANGPYRE WRECKING BALL

SNAKE TRICKS

LLOYD GARMADON TRIES to snatch the Fangpyre Staff, but the Serpents are one step ahead of him. To teach him a lesson, Fangdam activates the terrifying Fangpyre Wrecking Ball crane. Ninja to the rescue! Watch out for the swinging ball, biting jaws, and whipping tail.

NINJA FILE
- **SET NAME** FANGPYRE WRECKING BALL
- **SET NUMBER** 9457
- **YEAR** 2012
- **PIECES** 415

Flexible tail

Swinging spiked wrecking ball

Toolbox cabinet

Fangdam and a viper minion

Lloyd Garmadon wielding Lightning Bolt Staff

ARTICULATED ATTACK
The tail of the crane is jointed and fully articulated, so it can swing and bend in all directions. At the back of the crane there are two handy toolbox cabinets that can double up as a weapon store.

DID YOU KNOW?
When the Fangpyre snakes bite a vehicle, it gains snake-like abilities and a Serpentine appearance. The Fangpyre tribe provides most of the vehicles for the rest of the Serpent tribes.

Whip-like end to articulated tail

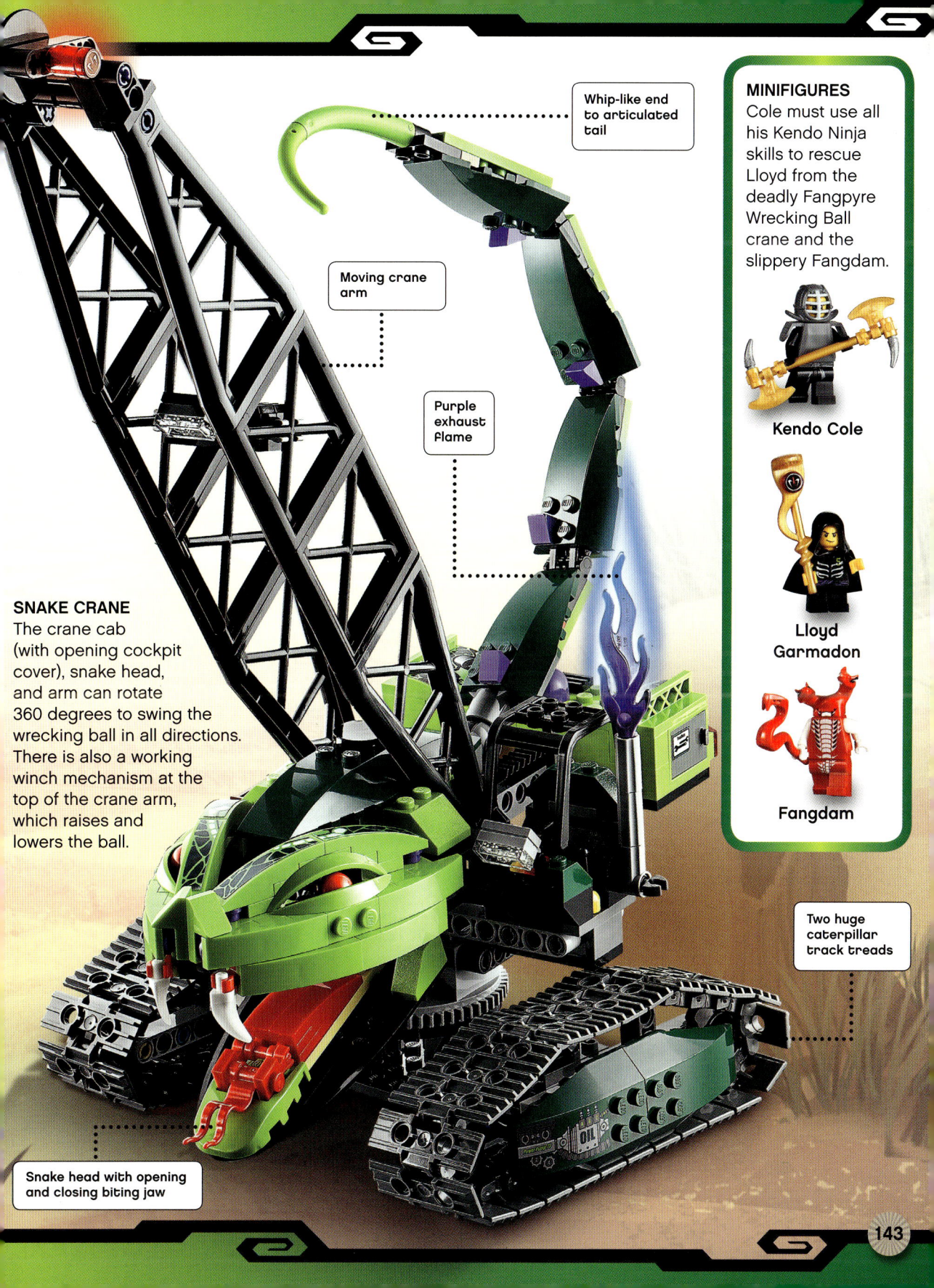

Moving crane arm

Purple exhaust flame

MINIFIGURES
Cole must use all his Kendo Ninja skills to rescue Lloyd from the deadly Fangpyre Wrecking Ball crane and the slippery Fangdam.

Kendo Cole

Lloyd Garmadon

Fangdam

SNAKE CRANE
The crane cab (with opening cockpit cover), snake head, and arm can rotate 360 degrees to swing the wrecking ball in all directions. There is also a working winch mechanism at the top of the crane arm, which raises and lowers the ball.

Two huge caterpillar track treads

Snake head with opening and closing biting jaw

143

FANG-SUEI

FANGPYRE SOLDIER

FANG-SUEI IS the strongest of the Fangpyre soldiers and is quick to act on orders. He is always hungry and if he hasn't eaten, anyone who gets in his way is likely to become a tasty snack! He can turn people and machines into snakes with one deadly bite.

- Unique snakeskin pattern on head
- Distinctive narrow red head and long neck
- Extra large poisonous fangs
- Unique necklace made from fangs

NINJA FILE

SET NAME	FANG-SUEI
SET NUMBER	9567
YEAR	2012
PIECES	11

DID YOU KNOW?
The Fangpyre are viper-like snakes. A poisonous bite from a Fangpyre can turn anything or anyone into a snake.

ACCIDENTAL BITE!
Hallucinating in the heat of a battle in a dry desert, Fang-Suei mistook Fangdam for the enemy and bit him. The poisonous bite caused Fangdam to grow a second head!

Banana can be used to trip up Ninja!

DEADLY SPINNER CROWN
With the Serpent-patterned crown on his Spinjitzu spinner, Fang-Suei can whip up a super vicious and poisonous tornado of Serpent Fire.

Fang-Suei's head is made from the same mold as Chokun's (p.157).

Red and black scale pattern on white torso

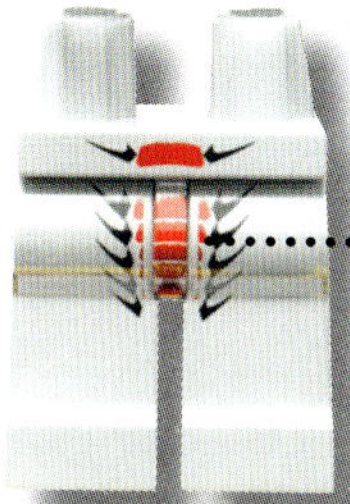

FRUITY
Fang-Suei always has a snack close at hand. He is so battle-focused he can turn anything into a weapon—even his lunch!

Red and black scales printed on white legs

Serpent spinner crown attachment

WEAPONS

CHAINED FANG
A dinosaur fang swung on the end of a steel chain is a deadly and accurate weapon.

GOLDEN VIPER
This golden viper minion helps its Fangpyre masters in battle.

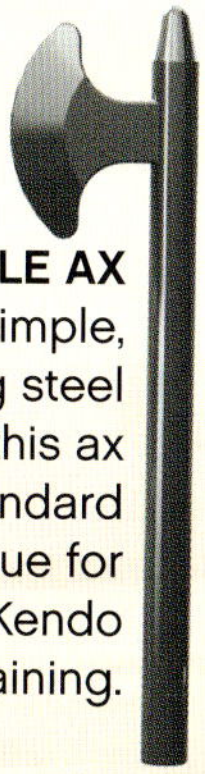

SUPER WARRIOR
Fang-Suei uses his strength in battle to wield two weapons at once. The golden point daggers are good for close combat or throwing.

BATTLE AX
With its simple, cutting steel power, this ax is standard issue for Kendo training.

Golden point dagger

Green spinner base

Serpentine symbols on Fang-Suei's fighting-red Spinjitzu spinner

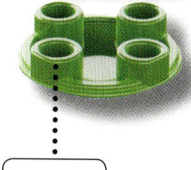

145

RATTLECOPTER
SKY WARS

WHO SAYS SNAKES can't fly? Fang-Suei corners Lloyd Garmadon with his mean, green, Ninja-fighting machine as the rebellious schoolboy tries to get away with the Constrictai Staff. The Rattlecopter poses a serious threat—Lloyd is in danger of being poisoned by lethal flick missiles or turned into a snake—unless Kai can come to his rescue...

Fire-powered jet pack

Missile tipped with poison

Tail handle for holding the copter as it flies

Secret viper missile launcher

Lloyd Garmadon wielding lightning bolt dagger

Constrictai Staff, exclusive to this set

SECRET SERPENT WEAPON
Fang-Suei's sly viper minions can be hidden in a cage at the back of the Rattlecopter. These poisonous snakes can then be dropped from the sky onto the enemy. Squeeze the two green side panels together at the point indicated by the arrows and launch Serpentine chaos!

Blades rotate 360 degrees for flying and hovering

BATTLE IN THE SKIES
This Serpent-themed helicopter is easy to fly. The rotating blades on top are specially angled down over the covered cockpit, so that you can hold the tail bar and maneuver the Rattlecopter to battle the enemies in the sky.

Fang-Suei slots into the cockpit to pilot the Rattlecopter.

Dual flick missile launcher

NINJA FILE
SET NAME	RATTLECOPTER
SET NUMBER	9443
YEAR	2012
PIECES	327

Rotating tail blade can also be used as crown attachment for spinners

Hinged blades can be moved in and out during flight

Powerful thrusters

Fang-Suei's vicious viper minion

Snake-like Rattlecopter face includes two hanging hinged fangs

MINIFIGURES
Kai swoops in on his jet pack to snatch the Constrictai Staff and rescue Lloyd before Fang-Suei sinks his fangs into the young Garmadon.

Kai ZX **Fang-Suei** **Lloyd Garmadon**

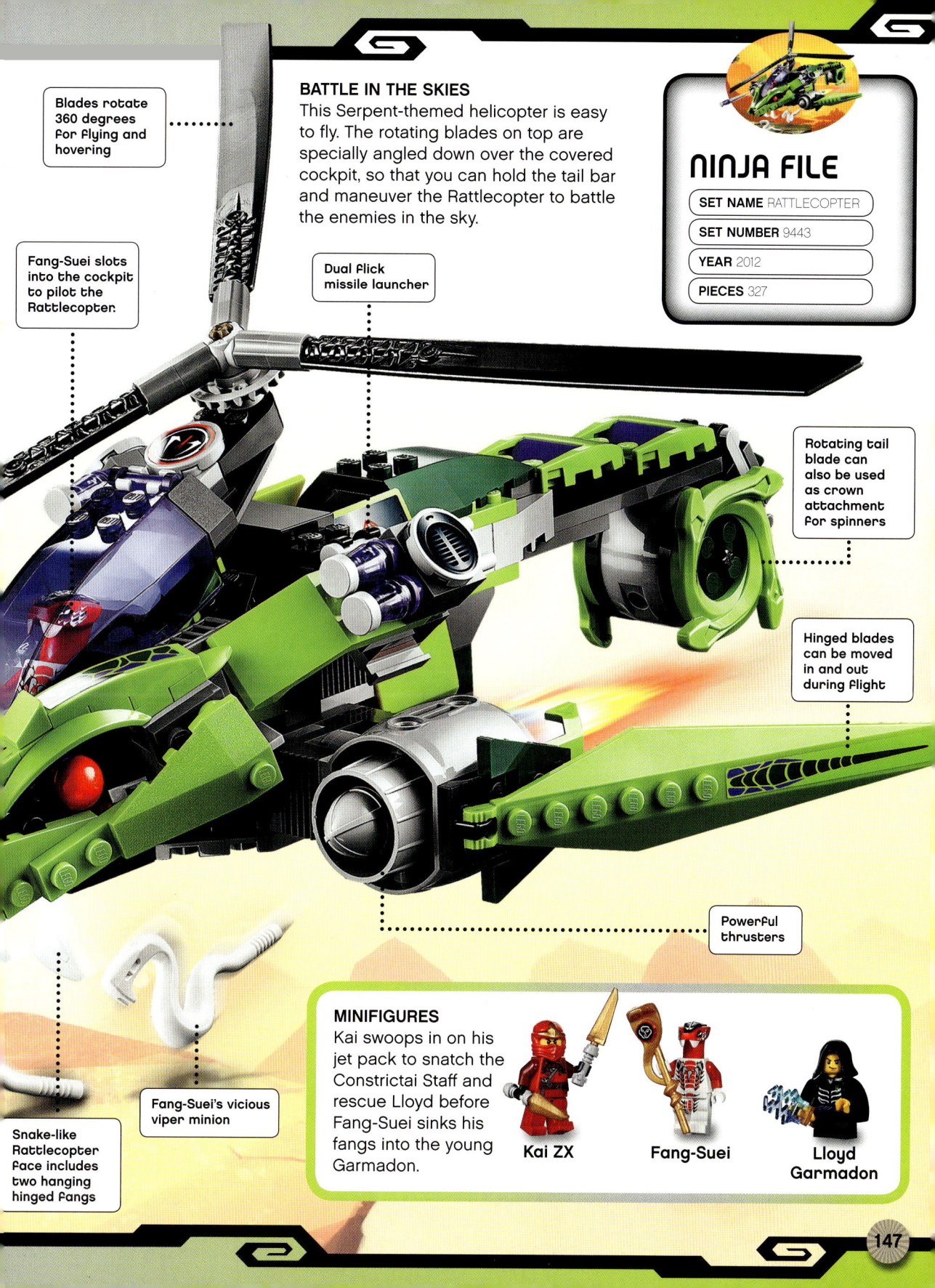

147

FANGPYRE MECH

SERPENT POWER

THE FANGPYRE MECH is Fang-Suei's terrifying Serpent battle robot. This massive mechanical monster is armed with fangs, grabbing hands, and a poison missile launcher—and it does whatever Fang-Suei tells him to. Get ready Cole, the Fangpyres are coming to get you!

Grabber hand can hold a minifigure

DID YOU KNOW?
The Mech and other Fangpyre vehicles were created when Fang-Suei and Snappa bit several ordinary broken-down vehicles.

Kendo Cole spins up a super Earth tornado.

MINIFIGURES
Cole battles Fang-Suei's mighty Mech monster with the Scythe of Quakes. Fang-Suei is armed with a banana!

Fang-Suei   Kendo Cole

Missile contains a vial of venom

FIRE AT WILL!
Slot the poisonous flick missile into the hole on the Mech's right arm and flick away. The Fangpyre venom will turn its victim into a snake-like creature.

KENDO COLE
Cole has now achieved his Kendo Ninja status. With his advanced martial arts and weapon skills, will Cole be strong enough to defeat this powerful and dangerous Serpentine machine? The mean Mech might have met its match!

Flick missile slots into right arm

Fang-Suei pilots the Mech from a cockpit behind the snake head.

Snake tail can swing from side to side on a ball joint

Large sharp fangs

Head, arms, legs, and feet are attached to ball joints to make them flexible

Don't trip on the banana!

NINJA FILE

SET NAME	FANGPYRE MECH
SET NUMBER	9455
YEAR	2012
PIECES	255

149

SNAPPA
FANGPYRE SCOUT

SNAPPA IS A scout and sniper in the Fangpyre tribe. He is a mean Serpent with a quick temper. Watch out—he usually bites first and worries about the consequences later. Of course, by then it is usually too late for his victims...

Viper-like snake headpiece fits onto regular minifigure head

Snake fangs

Fang necklace printed on torso

Snake scale pattern printed on torso and legs

Unusual all-white body

WEAPONS

TOOTH STAFF This staff is tipped with a fang to terrify the enemy.

GOLDEN SPEAR This valuable weapon is very rare.

SILVER DARK BLADE This sword is especially brutal in the hands of an evil Serpent.

MR. UNPOPULAR
Snappa is not the brainiest Serpent in the Fangpyre tribe, and he is certainly not the most popular. His hot temper and lack of brain power make it hard for the other snakes to like him.

NINJA FILE

SET NAME	SNAPPA
SET NUMBER	9564
YEAR	2012
PIECES	20

SKALES
HYPNOBRAI GENERAL

THIS COLD AND calculating snake warrior became leader of the Hypnobrai when he beat General Slithraa in a fight. Skales is one of the toughest Serpents and he is skilled in Fang-Kwon-Do, an ancient martial art.

DID YOU KNOW? There is no love lost between the Serpentine tribes. Yet at one time, the Hypnobrai and Fangpyre tribes were allies, so Skales is very good friends with Fangpyre General Fangtom.

Blue cobra-like hood with hypnotic pattern

Battle pike can grab and snap other weapons

NINJA FILE
SET NAME	COLE'S TREAD ASSAULT
SET NUMBER	9444
YEAR	2011
PIECES	286

DON'T MESS WITH THIS SNAKE! Skales is always looking for opportunities to fulfill his ambitions for control and power. He is so power-hungry that when the Serpentine leader, Pythor, disappears, Skales uses his snake cunning to make sure that he becomes the new ruler.

Before Skales became the Hypnobrai General, he had legs instead of a tail.

Scale pattern printed on torso and tailpiece.

SLITHRAA
EX HYPNOBRAI GENERAL

SLITHRAA WAS THE head of the Hypnobrai Serpent tribe until he was defeated by his second-in-command, Skales. After this humiliating incident, Slithraa lost his tail and grew legs again.

Unusual bright yellow markings on head

Cobra hood unique to the leaders of each Serpent tribe

Lethal snake fangs

Unique swirling snakeskin patterns on body

NINJA FILE
SET NAME	SLITHRAA
SET NUMBER	9573
YEAR	2012
PIECES	20

WEAPONS

HYPNOBRAI STAFF Owned by the General, this powerful Staff contains the anti-venom to reverse a hypnotic trance.

CHAIN SAI Swung from a chain, this three-pronged dagger is lethal.

BLUE VIPER A Hypnobrai minion snake uses mind control to confuse the enemy.

ICY SERPENTS The Hypnobrai are cobra-like snakes. The tribe was sealed away in the snowy mountains before Lloyd Garmadon accidentally released them. They use hypnosis to control their enemies.

RATTLA

HYPNOBRAI SCOUT

RATTLA IS THE scout for the Hypnobrai Army. He is not known for his brains, but he is loyal and follows orders. He has limited hypnotic powers, but his staff of control makes him very powerful in a fight.

WEAPONS

STAFF OF CONTROL
This staff fuses the powers of all weapons in its vicinity.

GOLDEN TRI SCYTHE
This is one of Rattla's most powerful weapons.

HYPNO VIPER
The rattle of the minion's tail causes mild hypnosis in its enemies.

- Unique snakeskin pattern begins on top of head
- Powerful red-eyed hypnotic stare
- Swirling patterns are distinctive of the Hypnobrai tribe.

SINGING SERPENT
Rattla likes to experiment with different ways of confusing his enemies—such as terrible singing or talking them to sleep with boring stories!

NINJA FILE

SET NAME	STARTER SET
SET NUMBER	9579
YEAR	2012
PIECES	62

MEZMO

HYPNOBRAI SOLDIER

MEZMO IS A soldier in the Hypnobrai tribe. He is smart and confident—if he doesn't agree with orders, he won't follow them. Mezmo feels he deserves more power in his tribe and should be promoted to a higher rank.

NINJA FILE
SET NAME	MEZMO
SET NUMBER	9555
YEAR	2012
PIECES	31

- Cobra-shaped head with Hypnobrai markings
- Hypnotic eyes
- Two large fangs
- Blue, yellow, and gray coloring matches other members of the tribe

WEAPONS

GOLDEN DOUBLE AX
This ultimate cutting weapon is made of solid gold!

- Golden ax blade

CHAINED FANG
Swing, strike, slice, and smash with this weapon!

PICKAX
This is a handy tool and a lethal weapon.

MESMERIZING!
Mezmo by name, mesmerizing by nature—just don't look into this snake's swirly red eyes. Like all Hypnobrai, he can hypnotize his enemies into doing whatever he wants.

SKALIDOR
CONSTRICTAI GENERAL

Super weapon—double-headed ax plus spear

Powerful arms with a boa-like grip

NINJA FILE
- **SET NAME** EPIC DRAGON BATTLE
- **SET NUMBER** 9450
- **YEAR** 2012
- **PIECES** 915

Distinctive spiked head

Long snake tail instead of legs

SKALIDOR IS the General of the Constrictai tribe. He is plump but powerful, and can crush his enemy with a single blow, or even with the weight of his own body! Ninja—don't be fooled by his size, Skalidor's reflexes are fast!

Black and orange scale pattern

UNDERGROUND FOE
The Constrictai Serpents live underground in caves and tunnels. When they move above ground the snakes are so heavy they make cracks in the earth—General Skalidor in particular!

BYTAR
CONSTRICTAI WARRIOR

THIS MUSCLE-BOUND warrior is second-in-command in the Constrictai tribe. Bytar is a bully who likes to work out when he isn't fighting. Unfortunately, he doesn't like to wash, so he smells B-A-D! Watch out Ninja, brutish Bytar eats and beats anything!

NINJA FILE
- **SET NAME** BYTAR
- **SET NUMBER** 9556
- **YEAR** 2012
- **PIECES** 25

WEAPONS

DOUBLE-BLADED SWORD
With this weapon, snakes can achieve twice as much cutting action!

SCYTHE BLADE
This is a lethal heavy metal weapon.

Sharp, curved silver blade

GOLDEN VIPER
Small, but with a mean grip, this viper minion works for the Constrictai.

Distinctive orange spikes on head

Large head with fangs

Vibrant snake scale pattern on torso

Large, muscular arms

VICE-LIKE GRIP
The Constrictai are boa constrictor snakes who attack their enemies from underground hideouts and crush them with their vice-like grips.

CHOKUN

CONSTRICTAI SOLDIER

CHOKUN IS A soldier and the protector of the Constrictai tribe. Don't be fooled by his small head, he has huge, sharp fangs. This snake has a killer bite!

Sinister, narrow head with gray and white scales

Large and venomous spiky fangs

Extra-long, powerful neck

NINJA FILE
SET NAME	WEAPON PACK
SET NUMBER	9591
YEAR	2012
PIECES	73

MOUNTAIN DWELLERS
Until their release by Lloyd Garmadon, the Constrictai tribe was sealed inside the tallest mountain in Ninjago.

WEAPONS

HAMMER
This tool is a heavy smashing weapon.

SILVER DARK BLADE
Snakes as well as Skeletons use this weapon.

SPEAR
This is a fast and target-precise weapon.

ORANGE VIPER
Eek!—A Constrictai minion!

All the Constrictai have short, stumpy legs.

SNIKE
CONSTRICTAI SCOUT

SNIKE IS A scout and a sniper in the Constrictai tribe. He is dedicated to his job, but he is slightly cross-eyed and doesn't always hit his targets at the first attempt. Despite this, Snike is confident and thinks he is a skilled sniper.

Regular head piece with boa attachment

NINJA FILE
- **SET NAME** SAMURAI MECH
- **SET NUMBER** 9448
- **YEAR** 2012
- **PIECES** 452

SHORT SNAKE
Snike is the same rank as the Fangpyre Snappa (p.150), but his minifigure has short, unposable legs. He appears in only one set (9448 Samurai Mech) and does not have his own spinner.

Constrictai Fang Blade

Snake Fangs

FANG BLADE
Snike helps Pythor get hold of the second of the four Fang Blades needed to release the Great Devourer.

Distinctive and unusual scale markings printed on orange torso

Short, unposable orange legs

PYTHOR
LAST OF THE ANACONDRAI

PYTHOR WAS GENERAL of the villainous Anacondrai, but now he is the tribe's last surviving member. He is the King of the Serpentine. Pythor wants all four Fang Blades so that he can release the Great Devourer and destroy Ninjago.

PRIDE COMES BEFORE A FALL!
When Pythor finally gets his hands on all four Fang Blades, he places them in the statue of the Great Devourer in order to release him from his tomb under the Lost City of Oroboris. His moment of triumph is short-lived—the first thing the Great Devourer does after his release is devour Pythor!

NINJA FILE
- **SET NAME** ULTRA SONIC RAIDER
- **SET NUMBER** 9449
- **YEAR** 2012
- **PIECES** 622

DID YOU KNOW?
Pythor, also known as Pythor P. Chumsworth, is exclusive to set 9449 (Ultra Sonic Raider). This set also features the ZX versions for the four Ninja and Spitta from the Venomari tribe.

- Open-mouthed head with four fangs is unique
- Scale pattern printed on uniquely purple torso, neck, and head
- Red vial of venom attached to handle of the Fangpyre Fang Blade
- Long snake tail typical of all Serpent Generals

159

SNAKE ARENA

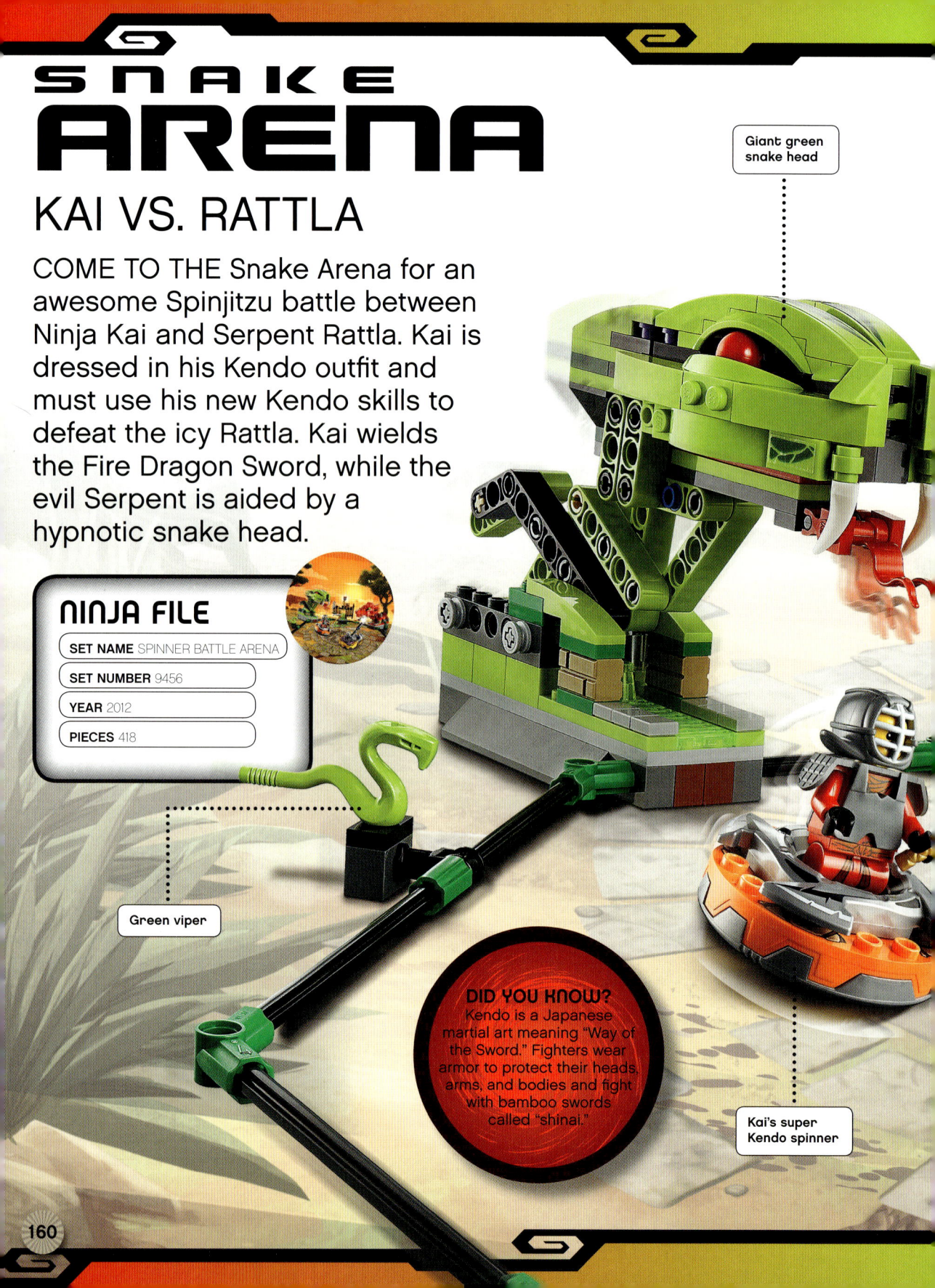

KAI VS. RATTLA

COME TO THE Snake Arena for an awesome Spinjitzu battle between Ninja Kai and Serpent Rattla. Kai is dressed in his Kendo outfit and must use his new Kendo skills to defeat the icy Rattla. Kai wields the Fire Dragon Sword, while the evil Serpent is aided by a hypnotic snake head.

NINJA FILE
- **SET NAME** SPINNER BATTLE ARENA
- **SET NUMBER** 9456
- **YEAR** 2012
- **PIECES** 418

Giant green snake head

Green viper

Kai's super Kendo spinner

DID YOU KNOW?
Kendo is a Japanese martial art meaning "Way of the Sword." Fighters wear armor to protect their heads, arms, and bodies and fight with bamboo swords called "shinai."

MINIFIGURES
Kendo Kai and Rattla battle it out one-on-one in the snake arena. Which weapons will they use and who will be the champion warrior?

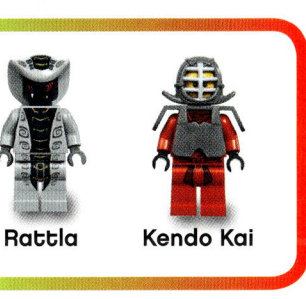

Rattla

Kendo Kai

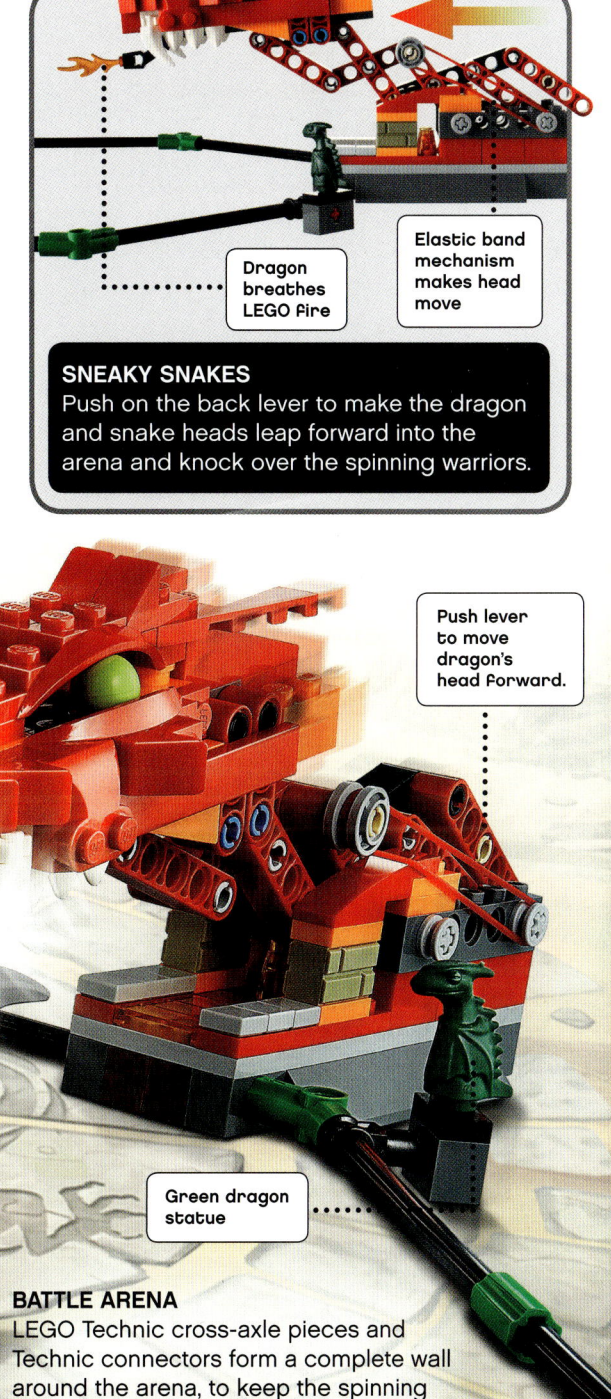

Snake Staff on weapon rack

Fire-breathing dragon head

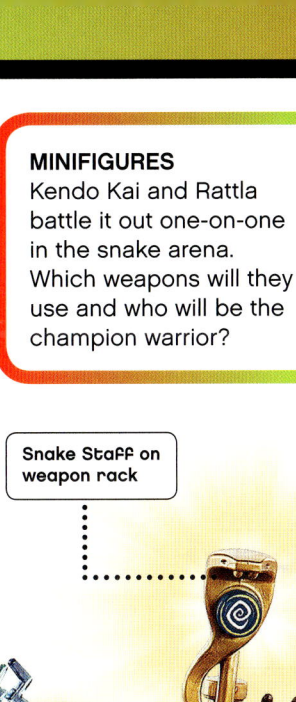

Dragon breathes LEGO fire

Elastic band mechanism makes head move

SNEAKY SNAKES
Push on the back lever to make the dragon and snake heads leap forward into the arena and knock over the spinning warriors.

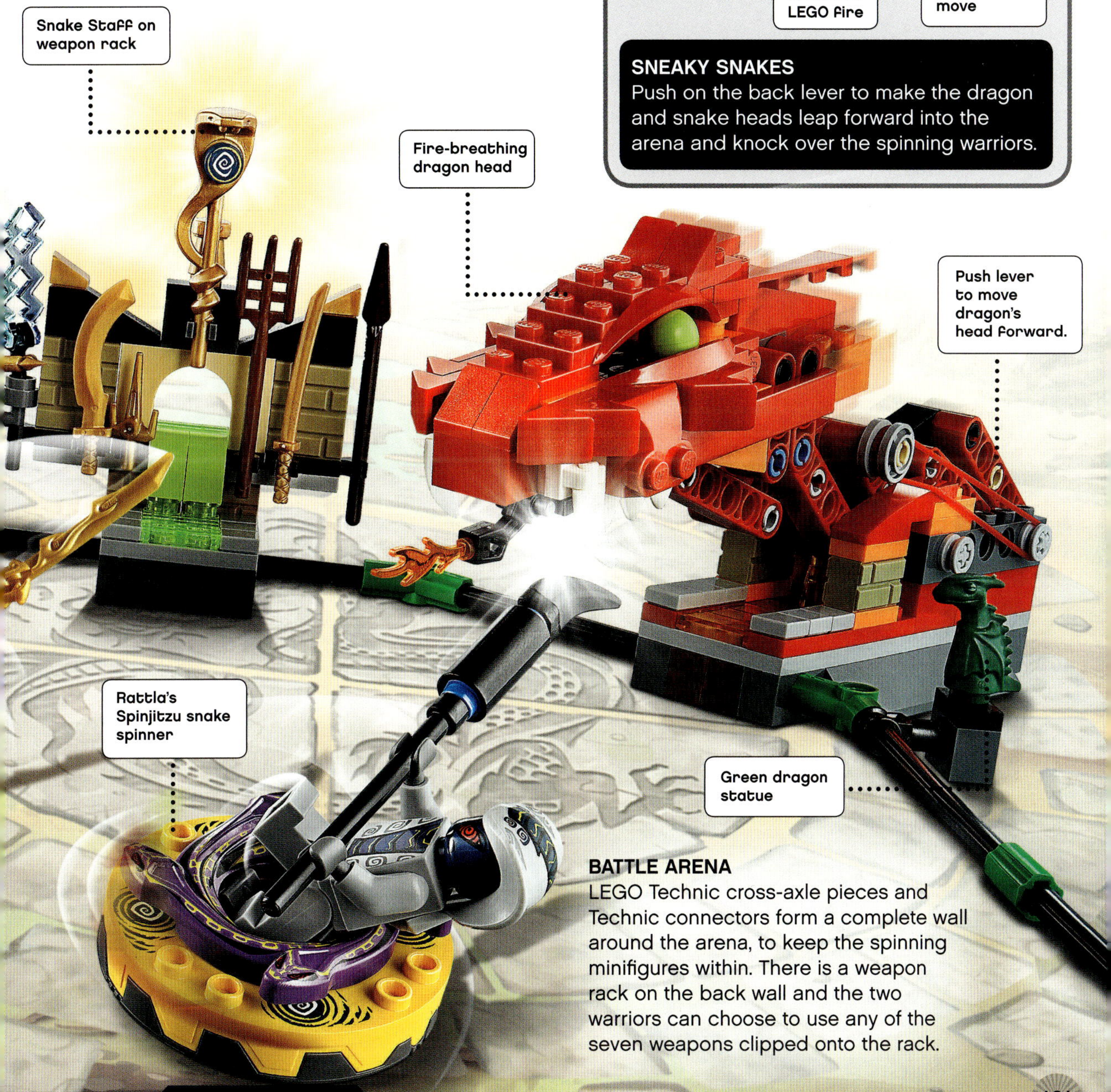

Push lever to move dragon's head forward.

Rattla's Spinjitzu snake spinner

Green dragon statue

BATTLE ARENA
LEGO Technic cross-axle pieces and Technic connectors form a complete wall around the arena, to keep the spinning minifigures within. There is a weapon rack on the back wall and the two warriors can choose to use any of the seven weapons clipped onto the rack.

EPIC DRAGON BATTLE

GOOD VS. EVIL

SENSEI WU HAS been captured by the Serpentine Army and the Great Devourer is on the loose. The Green Ninja and the Ultra Dragon—the most powerful of all Dragons—must defeat this evil beast, while Jay uses Zen skills to battle the snakes. Even Lord Garmadon is on the Ninja's side. Let battle commence!

Two golden vipers sit beside a venom fountain.

SNAKE PRISON
The Underworld Serpentine jail, where Sensei Wu is imprisoned, has front and back doors. Both doors can be opened, so that the Sensei Wu minifigure can be placed inside the prison cell.

Prison gate opens and closes

Black bridge moves up and down

Red spider comes with the set

Dripping venom

THE GREAT DEVOURER
The giant snake beast will consume all of Ninjago in its terrifying jaws if it is not stopped. Watch out, Ninja! The fang-filled mouth is big enough to hold a minifigure—before crushing and eating it!

Pull on green head flap to open and close jaws.

The Great Devourer's tail is posable.

Lethal snake fangs

NINJA FILE
SET NAME	EPIC DRAGON BATTLE
SET NUMBER	9450
YEAR	2012
PIECES	915

162

Handle moves wings up and down

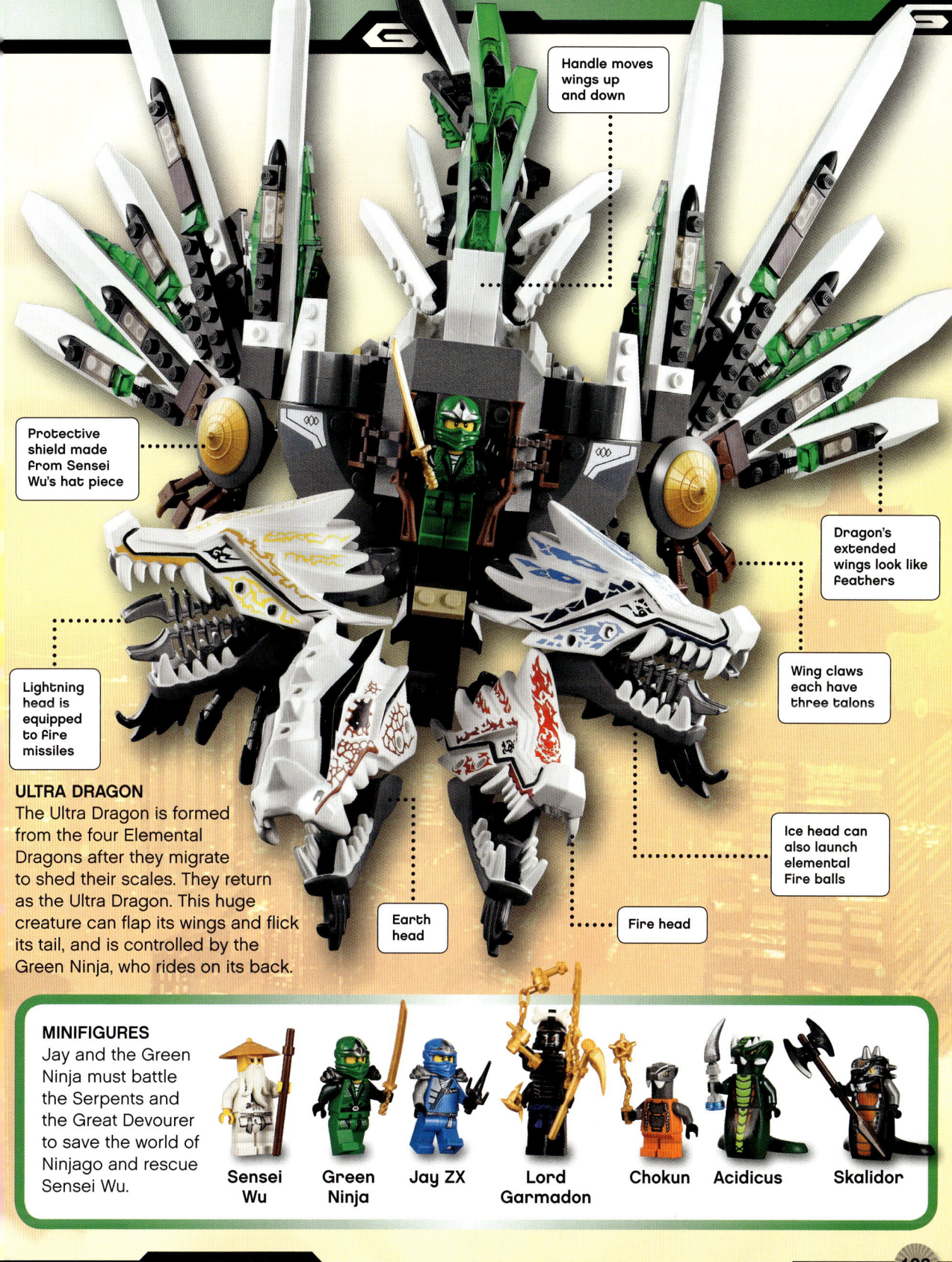

Protective shield made from Sensei Wu's hat piece

Dragon's extended wings look like feathers

Lightning head is equipped to fire missiles

Wing claws each have three talons

ULTRA DRAGON
The Ultra Dragon is formed from the four Elemental Dragons after they migrate to shed their scales. They return as the Ultra Dragon. This huge creature can flap its wings and flick its tail, and is controlled by the Green Ninja, who rides on its back.

Earth head

Fire head

Ice head can also launch elemental Fire balls

MINIFIGURES
Jay and the Green Ninja must battle the Serpents and the Great Devourer to save the world of Ninjago and rescue Sensei Wu.

Sensei Wu | Green Ninja | Jay ZX | Lord Garmadon | Chokun | Acidicus | Skalidor

WEAPONS

TAKE A LOOK at some fantastic weapons! Both the Ninja and the Serpentine use this amazing arsenal to attack their foes. While the Ninja prefer traditional swords, daggers, and, of course, their Golden Weapons, the Serpentine use a terrifying array of vile, venom-filled weapons.

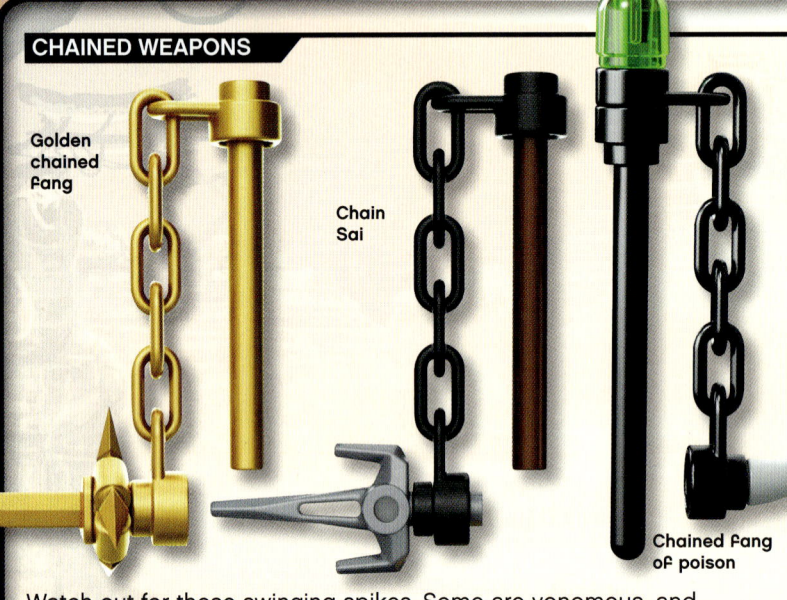

SWORDS AND KNIVES

Butterfly sword

Golden butterfly sword

Golden bowie knife

CHAINED WEAPONS

Golden chained fang

Chain Sai

Chained fang of poison

Watch out for these swinging spikes. Some are venomous, and some have more than one blade, but all of them are dangerous!

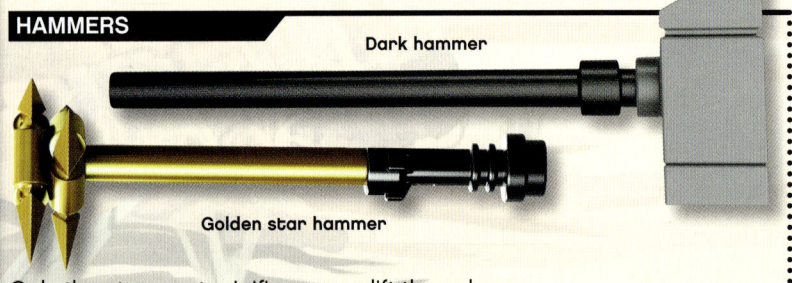

Golden chainsaw

HAMMERS

Dark hammer

Golden star hammer

Only the strongest minifigure can lift these heavy weapons, let alone do battle with them.

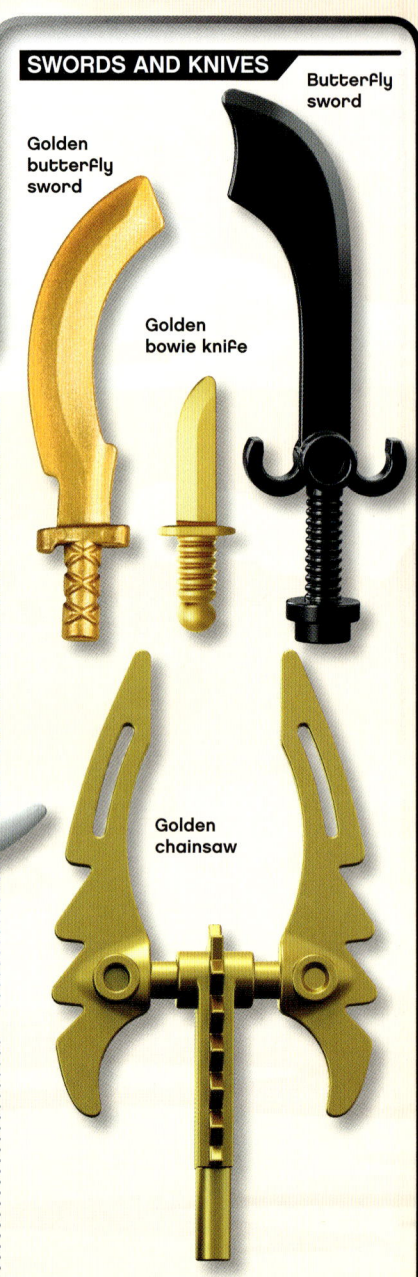

Don't underestimate these ornate blades—they're beautiful but also extremely sharp.

164

SCYTHES

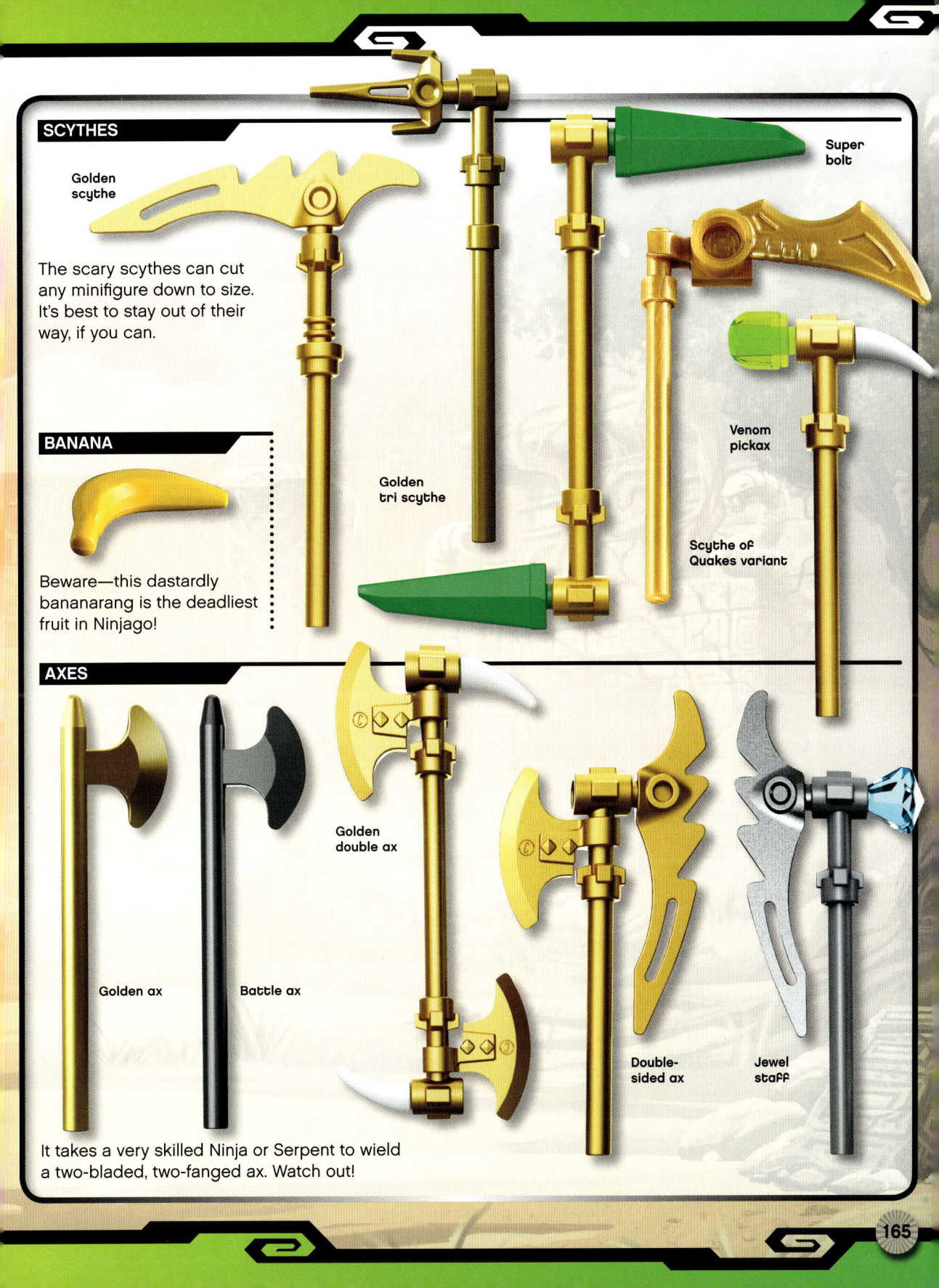

Golden scythe

The scary scythes can cut any minifigure down to size. It's best to stay out of their way, if you can.

Super bolt

Golden tri scythe

Venom pickax

Scythe of Quakes variant

BANANA

Beware—this dastardly bananarang is the deadliest fruit in Ninjago!

AXES

Golden ax

Battle ax

Golden double ax

Double-sided ax

Jewel staff

It takes a very skilled Ninja or Serpent to wield a two-bladed, two-fanged ax. Watch out!

165

STAFFS

Double-bladed battle ax

Double-bladed sword

Blinding staff

Golden staff of control

Trident

Golden Fangpyre Staff

Golden Constrictai Staff

Golden Venomari Staff

Golden Hypnobrai Staff

Gold-bladed saw staff

Staff of control

This impressive array of staffs wield many different powers. One has anti-venom to reverse hypnotic trances, another can blind its enemies, and a third can control all other weapons!

166

FANG BLADES

Made from pure silver and vials of anti-venom, these weapons are extremely powerful.

Hypnobrai Fang Blade

Constrictai Fang Blade

Fangpyre Fang Blade

Venomari Fang Blade

STRIKERS

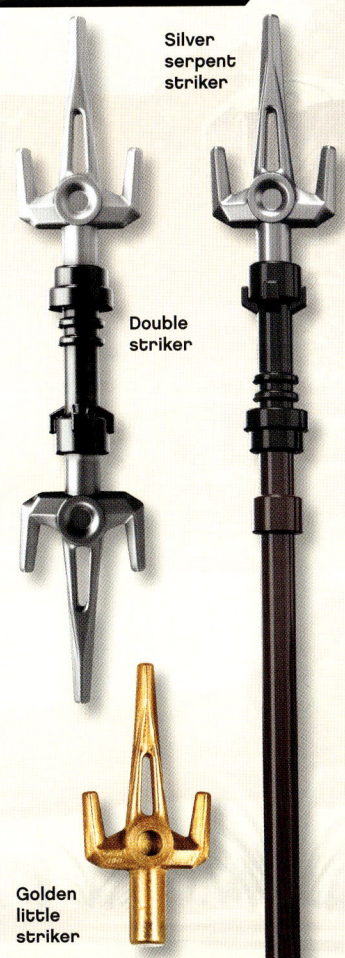

Silver serpent striker

Double striker

Golden little striker

These tri-pronged weapons can be used in close combat or thrown from a distance.

SPEARS

Battle Spear

Golden spear

Spear of fire

Dragon's breath spear

Spear of forked-tongues

This colorful collection of spears looks great, unless one of them is pointing right at you!

VIPERS

Toxic viper

Hypno viper

Golden viper

Sly viper

Whether they are shaking their noisy rattles, oozing with poison, or letting off smelly stink bombs, these slithery snake weapons are all ssscary!

167

ULTRA DRAGON VS. THE GREAT DEVOURER

AN EPIC BATTLE between good and evil is about to take place. The Serpents capture Sensei Wu, and finally unleash the Great Devourer. The Ninja call on the Green Ninja, the Ultra Dragon, and their enemy, Lord Garmadon, to help...

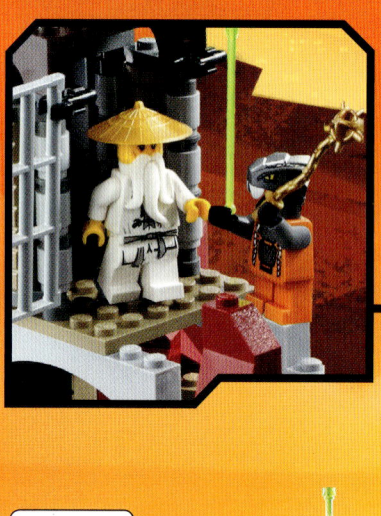

RESCUE! The Ninja find Sensei Wu. He tells them that Lloyd is the Green Ninja, and that Lloyd and Lord Garmadon are the only ones who can destroy the Great Devourer. Can either of them be trusted?

Lord Garmadon wields the four Golden Weapons.

Serpentine prison cell

HERO! The Green Ninja arrives with the Ultra Dragon to join the battle. The Ninja combine their elemental powers to control the Great Devourer just long enough for Garmadon to deliver the fatal blow with the four Golden Weapons. So long, snake!

Only the Green Ninja can control the Ultra Dragon.

DONE! The Great Devourer is destroyed and Ninjago is saved! But Garmadon has disappeared with the Golden Weapons. Has he gone back over to the Underworld? Only time will tell...

AND BEYOND...

HAVING DEFEATED THE Skeleton Army and the Serpentine, the Ninja will soon be ready to face a new challenge. In the meantime, turn the page to discover all the information you could ever need about all the LEGO® Ninjago sets and minifigures. Go in peace Ninja warrior!

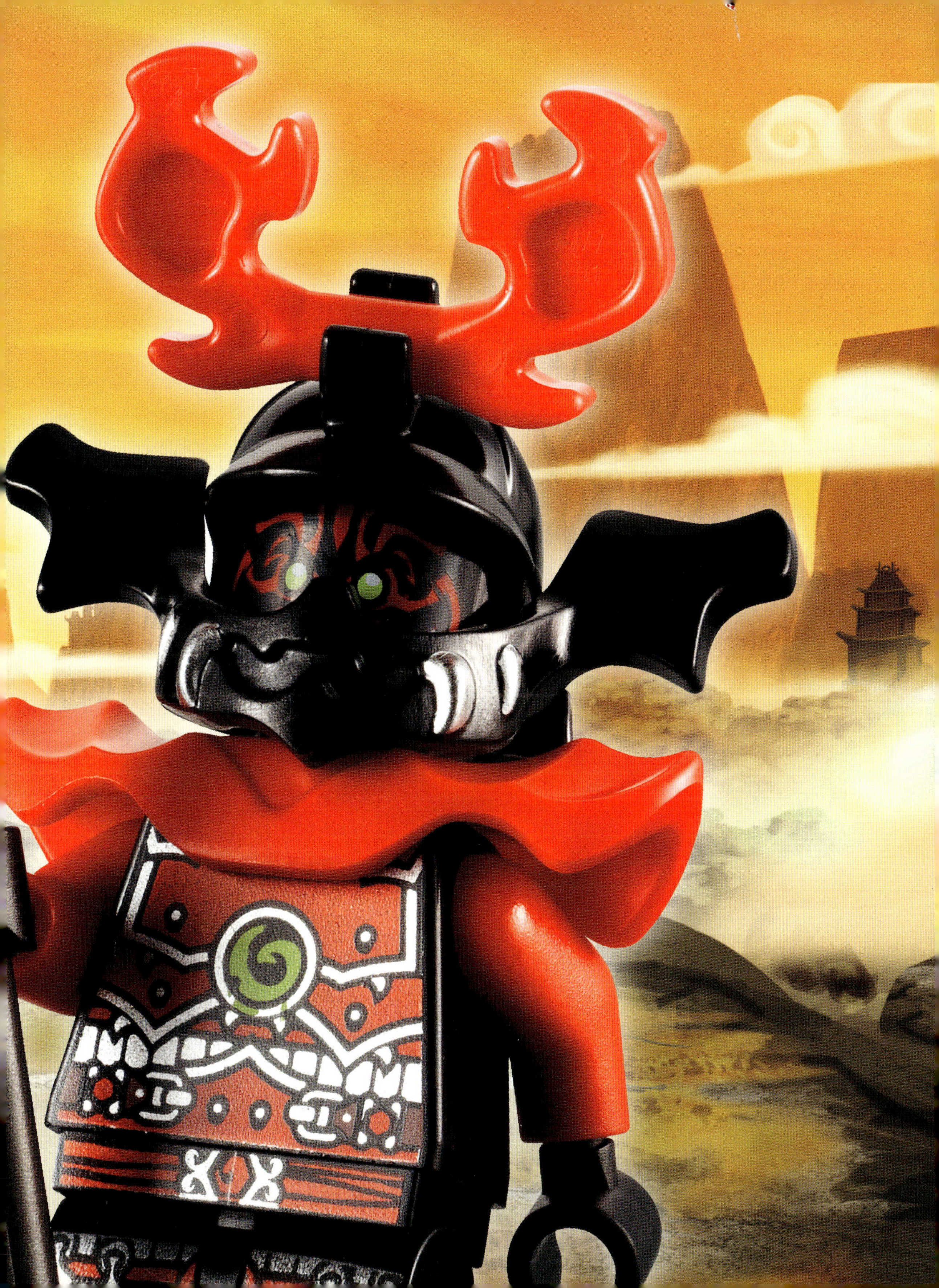

MINIFIGURE GALLERY

WHO IS YOUR favorite LEGO Ninjago minifigure? Is it Nya with her double-sided face, the two-headed Fangtom and Fangdam, or the super-short Lloyd Garmadon? Check out this line-up of all the amazing minifigures and make your choice!

Kai	Zane	Jay	Cole
Sensei Wu	Nya	Lord Garmadon	Samukai
Wyplash	Bonezai	Kruncha	Frakjaw
Nuckal	Krazi	Chopov	Sensei Wu DX
Kai DX	Zane DX	Jay DX	Cole DX

Green Ninja ZX (DK exclusive)

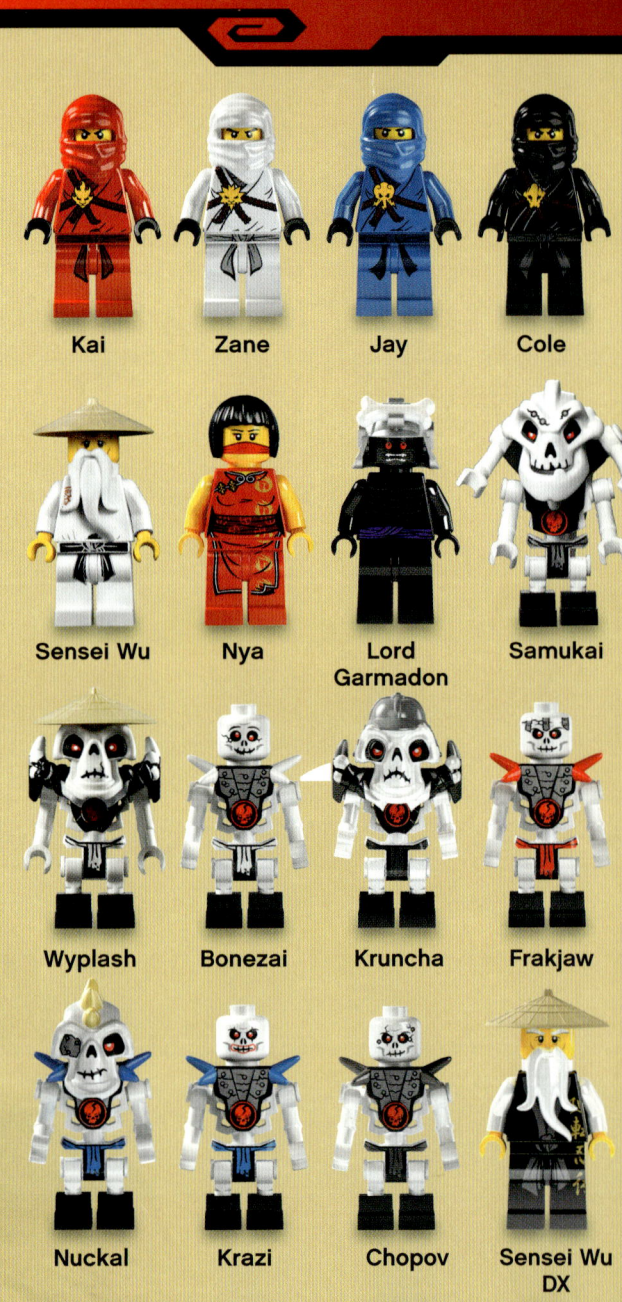

SEASON 1: NINJA VS. SKELETONS

172

| Sensei Wu | Kai ZX | Zane ZX | Jay ZX | Cole ZX | Green Ninja | Samurai X | Lloyd Garmadon |

| Kendo Kai | Kendo Zane | Kendo Jay | Kendo Cole | NRG Kai | NRG Zane | NRG Jay | NRG Cole |

| Acidicus | Lasha | Lizaru | Spitta | Fangtom | Fangdam | Fang-Suei |

| Snappa | Skales | Slithraa | Rattla | Mezmo |

| Skalidor | Snike | Chokun | Bytar | Pythor | Lord Garmadon |

SEASON 2: NINJA VS. SERPENTINES

173

SET GALLERY

HERE ARE ALL the LEGO® Ninjago sets produced so far in each series. How many sets have you collected? Which one is your favorite? Look out for even more sets coming in 2013!

2516 Ninja Training Outpost

2507 Fire Temple

2519 Skeleton Bowling

2509 Earth Dragon Defence

2263 Turbo Shredder

2518 Nuckal's ATV

2505 Garmadon's Dark Fortress

2521 Lightning Dragon Battle

2260 Ice Dragon Attack

2504 Spinjitzu Dojo

2506 Skull Truck

2254 Mountain Shrine

2259 Skull Motorbike

2258 Ninja Ambush

2520 Ninjago Battle Arena

2508 Blacksmith Shop

SEASON 1: NINJA VS. SKELETONS

174

9440 Venomari Shrine

9441 Kai's Blade Cycle

9456 Spinner Battle

9447 Lasha's Bite Cycle

9442 Jay's Storm Fighter

9443 Rattlecopter

9455 Fangpyre Mech

9448 Samurai Mech

9446 Destiny's Bounty

9457 Fangpyre Wrecking Ball

9449 Ultra Sonic Raider

9444 Cole's Tread Assault

9445 Fangpyre Truck Ambush

9450 Epic Dragon Battle

SEASON 2: NINJA VS. SERPENTINE

EXCLUSIVE MINIFIGURE

This unique minifigure has been specially created for DK by the LEGO Group. It is the Green Ninja, aka Lloyd Garmadon, wearing an exclusive green, black, and gold outfit. Put him together and let your Ninja adventures begin!

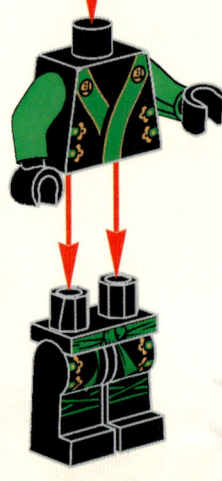

ACKNOWLEDGMENTS

Dorling Kindersley would like to thank Corinna Van Delden, Michael Thejl Nielsen, Randi Sørensen, Helle Reimers Holm-Jørgensen, Pat M. Madsen, Nelson LaMonica, Jane Puggaard Hougaard, Thomas Kristensen, Menelaos Florides, Samuel Thomas Johnson, Adrian Florea, and Kurt Meysmans at the LEGO Group.

DK

LONDON, NEW YORK, MUNICH, MELBOURNE, AND DELHI

Editors Shari Last, Emma Grange, Julia March
Editorial Assistant Ruth Amos
Designers Lauren Rosier, Mark Richards, Jon Hall
Project Art Editor Clive Savage
Design Manager Ron Stobbart
Publishing Manager Catherine Saunders
Art Director Lisa Lanzarini
Publisher Simon Beecroft
Publishing Director Alex Allan
Pre-Production Producer Andy Hilliard
Senior Producer Melanie Mikellides

First published in the United States in 2012
by DK Publishing
375 Hudson Street
New York, New York 10014
10 9 8 7 6 5 4 3 2 1
LEGO, the LEGO logo, and the Minifigure are trademarks of the LEGO Group.
© 2012 the LEGO Group.
Produced by Dorling Kindersley under license from the LEGO Group.

001—185656—Nov/12

All rights reserved under International and Pan-American Copyright Conventions. No part of this publication may be reproduced, stored in a retrieval system, or transmitted in any form or by any means, electronic, mechanical, photocopying, recording, or otherwise, without the prior written permission of the copyright owner.
Published in Great Britain by Dorling Kindersley Limited.

DK books are available at special discounts when purchased in bulk for sales promotions, premiums, fund-raising, or educational use.

For details, contact:
DK Publishing Special Markets
375 Hudson Street
New York, New York 10014
SpecialSales@dk.com

A catalog record for this book is available from the Library of Congress.

ISBN: 978-0-7566-9812-6

Color reproduction by Media Development and Printing, UK
Printed and bound by Leo Paper Products, China

Discover more at
www.dk.com
www.LEGO.com